EXPERIENCING PSYCHOLOGY

Active Learning Adventures

Gary G. Brannigan

State University of New York–Plattsburgh

Prentice Hall
Upper Saddle River, New Jersey 07458

Library of Congess Cataloging-in-Publication

Brannigan, Gary G.
    Experiencing psychology: active learning adventures/Gary
Brannigan.
      p.   cm.
    Includes bibliographical references.
    ISBN 0-32-103282-9
    1. Psychology Problems, exercises, etc.   I.Title
BF121.B635 2000
150'.76—dc21

99-32702
CIP

Editor-in-Chief: *Nancy Roberts*
Executive Editor: *Bill Webber*
Assistant Editor: *Jennifer Cohen*
Managing Editor: *Mary Rottino*
Production Liaison: *Fran Russello*
Production Editor: *Kerry Reardon*
Prepress and Maufacturing Buyer: *Tricia Kenny*
Cover Design: *Bruce Kenselaar*
Cover Director: *Jayne Conte*

© 2000 Prentice Hall
Upper Saddle River, NJ 07458

This book was set in 12/14 Times New Roman
and was printed and bound by Victor Graphics.

Printed in the United States of America

10 9 8 7 6 5 4 3 2 1

ISBN 0-32-103282-9

Prentice-Hall International (UK) Limited, *London*
Prentice-Hall of Australia Pty. Limited, *Sydney*
Prentice-Hall Canada Inc., *Toronto*
Prentice-Hall Hispanoamericana, S.A., *Mexico*
Prentice-Hall of India Private Limited, *New Delhi*
Prentice-Hall of Japan, Inc., *Tokyo*
Pearson Education Asia Pte. Ltd., *Singapore*
Editora Prentice-Hall do Brasil, Ltda., *Rio de Janeiro*

CONTENTS

ABOUT THE AUTHOR

Gary G. Brannigan (Ph.D., University of Delaware) is a Professor of Psychology at SUNY–Plattsburgh and a fellow of the Society for Personality Assessment. He also served as Director of the Psychological Services Clinic at SUNY–Plattsburgh and was a consultant to several local agencies. His research focuses primarily on psychological assessment and therapy with children. He is currently serving on the editorial boards of two journals. In addition to coediting *The Undaunted Psychologist: Adventures in Research*, *The Social Psychologists: Research Adventures*, *The Developmental Psychologists: Research Adventures Across the Life Span*, and *The Sex Scientists*, and editing *The Enlightened Educator: Research Adventures in the Schools*, and *The Sport Scientists: Research Adventures,* he has published numerous articles, chapters, books, and tests, including *Research and Clinical Applications of the Bender-Gestalt Test*, *Experiences in Personality: Research, Assessment, and Change*, and *The Modified Version of the Bender-Gestalt Test* (now in its second edition).

PREFACE

Experiencing Psychology: Active Learning Adventures contains thirty-nine active learning experiences that correspond to major topics covered in introductory psychology:

Research Design	Motivation and Emotion
Biopsychology	Development
Sensation and Perception	Personality
Consciousness	Psychological Disorders
Learning	Therapies
Memory	Social Psychology
Language, Thinking, and Intelligence	

The activities can be used to supplement instruction and enhance learning by providing students with opportunities to explore theories and concepts in psychology. Although they are designed as out-of-classroom assignments, the activities are rich with possibilities for in-class use. For example, you can collate students' responses, develop class norms, and compare, contrast, and discuss responses in large or small group formats. Students generally enjoy this approach because they are not merely passive recipients of knowledge. Rather, they come to class armed with first-hand experience in the subject matter.

You should feel free to adjust activities to suit the needs of your course (e.g., adding, deleting, or modifying questions). In fact, I would appreciate your suggestions for improving any of the activities. I can be reached at the Department of Psychology, State University of New York–Plattsburgh, Plattsburgh, New York 12901 (e-mail: Gary.Brannigan@plattsburgh.edu).

Acknowledgments

I deeply appreciate the assistance of Rebecca Pascal, Adam Rodnitzky, Bill Webber, Jennifer Cohen, Kerry Reardon, and Brenda Melissaratos. Their counsel and support enhanced the quality of this book. The reviewers also provided valuable suggestions for clarifying and improving activities. I greatly appreciate the efforts of David P. Nalbone, T. L. Brink, Brenda Riemer, Debra Lee Hollister, Jack Kapeller, Jessica Miller, Michael Casey, Gregory Cutler, and Carol A. Hayes.

I am grateful to the State University of New York–Plattsburgh for providing the supportive environment that enabled me to pursue this project. The advice, help, and support of my colleagues, especially Cindy Lightfoot, Jeanne Ryan, and Nancy Elwess, were invaluable. I also wish to thank the many students who helped to field test these activities. Their suggestions made the book more student-focused and accessible.

My friend and secretary, Judy Dashnaw, contributed immensely to the quality of this book. Her superior skills in editing, formatting, and word processing, as well as her dedication to excellence, were indispensable.

Finally, I wish to thank my wife, Linda, for her ongoing support. She plays a major role in everything I do.

INTRODUCTION

It's one thing to "read" psychology; it's quite another to "do" psychology. Although textbooks generally do a good job of transmitting basic information, they tell us very little about the important decision-making processes used to collect that information. As Arthur Combs noted in *The Future Demands of Education* (1981), this must change. "Effective problem solving is learned by confronting events, defining problems, puzzling with them, experimenting, trying, searching for effective solutions" (p. 370). This orientation is further emphasized in the following story about Richard Feynman (1988), the Nobel prize–winning scientist.

One day, I was playing with an "express wagon," a little wagon with a railing around it. It had a ball in it, and when I pulled the wagon, I noticed something about the way the ball moved. I went to my father and said, "Say, Pop, I noticed something. When I pulled the wagon, the ball rolls to the back of the wagon. And when I'm pulling it along and I suddenly stop, the ball rolls to the front of the wagon. Why is that?"

"That, nobody knows," he said. "The general principle is that things which are moving tend to keep on moving, and things which are standing still tend to stand still, unless you push them hard. This tendency is called 'inertia,' but nobody knows why it's true." Now, that's a deep understanding. He didn't just give me the name.

He went on to say, "If you look from the side, you'll see that it's the back of the wagon that you're pulling against the ball, and the ball stands still. As a matter of fact, from the friction it starts to move forward a little bit in relation to the ground. It doesn't move back."

I ran back to the little wagon and set the ball up again and pulled the wagon. Looking sideways, I saw that indeed he was right. Relative to the sidewalk, it moved forward a little bit.

That's the way I was educated by my father, with examples and discussions: no pressure—just lovely, interesting discussions. It has motivated me for the rest of my life, and makes me interested in *all* the sciences. (It just happens I do physics better.)

I've been caught, so to speak—like someone who was given something wonderful when he was a child, and he's always looking for it again. I'm always looking, like a child, for the wonders I know I'm going to find— maybe not every time, but every once in a while (pp. 15-16). [From "What do you care what other people think?": Further adventures of a curious character by Richard P. Feynman as told to Ralph Leighton. Copyright © 1988 by Gweneth Feynman and Ralph Leighton. Reprinted by permission of W. W. Norton & Company, Inc.]

My first attempt to achieve the goal of involving students in psychology resulted in several books (see References) that revolved around first-person accounts of how and why scientists do what they do. Although the stories provided interesting details about the personal and professional factors that influence scientists' work, as well as in-depth coverage of major research projects, I noted that they were no substitute for first-hand experience.

This is my second attempt to reach this goal (and my second book of this type—see References). The activities are designed to involve you in the excitement of discovery and allow you to personally explore the theories and concepts you encounter in psychology. You will not only think about but also participate in the topics you study. This will make the process of learning more dynamic and meaningful and will give you a clearer understanding of yourself and the world around you.

Throughout the book, you will be collecting data on yourself and others. When you use other people as subjects, you or your instructor will likely need to receive permission from a special campus committee established to protect human subjects. When you complete an experiment, be sure to adhere strictly to their guidelines; thoroughly "debrief" your subject about the nature of the experiment and answer all of his or her questions.

Finally, in addition to being interesting, informative, and challenging, the activities should be fun. Enjoy your adventures.

References

Brannigan, G. G. (Ed.) (1996). *The enlightened educator: Research adventures in the schools*. New York: McGraw-Hill.

Brannigan, G. G. (Ed.) (1999). *The sport scientists: Research adventures*. New York: Longman.

Brannigan, G. G., Allgeier, E. R., & Allgeier, A. R. (Eds.) (1998). *The sex scientists*. New York: Longman.

Brannigan, G. G., & Merrens, M. R. (Eds.) (1993). *The undaunted psychologist: Adventures in research*. New York: McGraw-Hill

Brannigan, G. G., & Merrens, M. R. (Eds.) (1995). *The social psychologists: Research adventures*. New York: McGraw-Hill.

Combs, A. W. (1981). The future demands of education. *Phi Delta Kappa, 62,* 369-372.

Feynman, R. P. (1988*). What do you care what other people think? Further adventures of a curious character*. New York: Norton.

Merrens, M. R., & Brannigan, G. G. (Eds.) (1996). *The developmental psychologists: Research adventures across the life span*. New York: McGraw-Hill.

Merrens, M. R., & Brannigan, G. G. (1998). *Experiences in personality: Research, assessment, and change*. New York: Wiley.

CHAPTER 1

INTRODUCTION TO PSYCHOLOGY

Name _____

Date _____

ACTIVE LEARNING EXPERIENCE

1.1 PERSONAL THEORY

Whether or not people study psychology, they develop theories about human behavior. People appear to have a need to categorize people and events to "make sense" of the world.

The following activity, based on Kenneth Kerber's (1987) exercise, should give you an idea about your personal theory of human behavior before you begin your formal study of psychology. Examine the following concepts and check the three that are most important to your understanding of your "self" and your behavior.

Concepts

_____ 1.   Unconscious Motives (motives that one is unaware of)

_____ 2.   Finding Meaning in Life

_____ 3.   Habits

_____ 4.   Future Expectations

_____ 5.   Autonomy (independent, self-regulating)

_____ 6.   Thought Patterns (how one interprets experiences)

_____ 7.   Heredity

_____ 8.   Early Childhood Experiences

_____ 9.   External Circumstances

_____ 10. Traits (characteristics that one displays in most situations)

_____ 11. Beliefs

_____ 12. Rewards and Punishments

_____ 13. Defense Mechanisms (strategies used to protect the self from anxiety, shame, or guilt)

_____ 14. Self-actualization (inborn drive to develop one's potential)

_____ 15. Unchangeability

Explain why you chose each concept that you checked.

How do they fit together to form your personal theory of human behavior?

Note that the 15 concepts can be broken down into the major theories in psychology.

Theory		Items
Psychoanalytic	:	1, 8, and 13
Behavioral	:	3, 9, and 12
Humanistic	:	2, 5, and 14
Cognitive	:	4, 6, and 11
Trait	:	7, 10, and 15

Does your theory fit with some theories better than others? Explain.

As you progress through your course in psychology, you will see how each of these theories contributes to our understanding of human behavior.

Reference

Kerber, K. W. (19897). What is personality? A personal appraisal. In V. P. Makosky, L. G. Whittemore, & A. M. Rogers (Eds.). *Activities handbook for the teaching of psychology* (Vol. 2) (pp. 182–184). Washington, DC: American Psychological Association.

Name _____

Date _____

ACTIVE LEARNING EXPERIENCE

1.2 EXPERIMENTAL DESIGN

Bernardi Carducci (1990) produced an interesting activity to introduce some of the basic principles of research methodology. The activity stems from the belief held by some students that speaking in class will "kill" them.

Given the human resources in your classroom, design an experiment to test this belief: **Actively participating in class will kill you**.

1.   What is your hypothesis?

2.   How would you select your subjects?

3.   What is your independent variable? Give a detailed description of the experimental procedure you would follow.

4.   What is your dependent variable?

5.   What are the limitations of your experiment?

Reference

Carducci, B. J. (1990). Will class participation "kill" you? Refuting a common irrational belief by teaching research methods. In V. P. Makosky, C. C. Seteo, L. G. Whittermore, C. P. Landry, & M. L. Skutley (Eds.). *Activities handbook for the teaching of psychology* (Vol. 3) (pp. 203-205). Washington, DC: American Psychological Association.

CHAPTER 2

BIOPSYCHOLOGY

Name _____

Date _____

ACTIVE LEARNING EXPERIENCE

2.1   REACTION TIME

Reaction time experiments have a long history in psychology. Through these experiments, psychologists have been able to examine a wide variety of processes, from simple repetitive reactions to complex mental operations.

In this activity, you will have an opportunity to assess reaction time to three tasks. The activity requires a deck of playing cards (actually only the numbered cards ace through 10—not the face cards), a stopwatch, and a volunteer to serve as your subject.

For each of the three tasks, your subject should be seated in a straight back chair at a table or desk.

Task 1

Shuffle the 40 cards (aces through 10's) and hand the deck face down to the subject. Instruct the subject to turn the cards over one by one and place them face up in a *single* pile on the table/desk as quickly as possible. Ask the subject if he/she understands the directions and when he/she is ready, say "Begin" and start your stopwatch.

Record the time it takes the subject to complete the task and note any errors.

Time _____

Errors ____

Task 2

Shuffle the cards and hand the deck face down to the subject. Instruct the subject to turn the cards over one by one and place them in a *single* pile with the red cards (diamonds and hearts) facing up and the black cards (spades and clubs) facing down. Make sure the subject understands the directions and when he/she is ready, say "Begin" and start your stopwatch.

Record the time it takes the subject to complete the task and note any errors.

Time _____

Errors ____

Task 3

Rearrange the cards so they all face the same way and shuffle the deck. Hand the deck face down to the subject. Instruct the subject to turn the cards over one by one and place them in a *single* pile with diamonds facing up in the vertical direction, clubs facing down in the vertical direction, hearts facing up in the horizontal direction, and spades facing down in the horizontal direction. Make sure the subject understands the directions, and demonstrate the positions if necessary. When the subject is ready, say "Begin" and start your stopwatch.

Record the time it takes the subject to complete the task and note any errors.

Time _____

Errors ____

If you noted differences in time and/or errors across tasks, how would you explain them from a neuropsychological standpoint? What neuropsychological abilities would be required for each task?

Task 1

Task 2

Task 3

Name _____

Date _____

ACTIVE LEARNING EXPERIENCE

2.2 HEMISPHERIC PREFERENCE

In recent years there has been increased speculation about brain localization and cerebral hemispheric dominance. Rudolph Wagner and Kelly Wells (1985) developed the following inventory to assess neurobehavioral left/right dominance. [From A refined neurobehavioral inventory of hemispheric preference. *Journal of Clinical Psychology, 41*, 671-676. Copyright © 1985. Reprinted with permission of John Wiley & Sons, Inc.]

Instructions: Read the statements carefully. There are 12 statements with four items each. Place a cross mark (X) in the appropriate bracket in front of each item you select. Mark **one item** only under each of the 12 statements. Choose the activity you **prefer** even though it does not necessarily mean that you have the **ability** to do it. If you are undecided, make a decision anyway by guessing.

1. ( ) a. Major in logic
   ( ) b. Write a letter
   ( ) c. Fix things at home
   ( ) d. Major in art

2. ( ) a. Be a movie critic
   ( ) b. Learn new words
   ( ) c. Improve your skills in a game
   ( ) d. Create a new toy

3. ( ) a. Improve your strategy in a game
   ( ) b. Remember people's names
   ( ) c. Engage in sports
   ( ) d. Play an instrument by ear

4. ( ) a. Review a book
   ( ) b. Write for a magazine
   ( ) c. Build new shelves at home
   ( ) d. Draw a landscape or seascape

5. ( ) a. Analyze market trends
   ( ) b. Write a movie script
   ( ) c. Do carpentry work
   ( ) d. Imagine a new play

6. ( ) a. Analyze management practices
   ( ) b. Locate words in a dictionary
   ( ) c. Put jigsaw puzzles together
   ( ) d. Paint in oil

7. ( ) a. Be in charge of computer programming
    ( ) b. Study word origins and meaning
    ( ) c. Putter in the yard
    ( ) d. Invent a new gadget

8. ( ) a. Analyze production cost
    ( ) b. Describe a new product in words
    ( ) c. Sell a new product on the market
    ( ) d. Draw a picture of a new product

9. ( ) a. Explain the logic of a theory
    ( ) b. Be a copy writer for ads
    ( ) c. Work with wood and clay
    ( ) d. Invent a story

10. ( ) a. Be a comparison shopper
    ( ) b. Read about famous men and women
    ( ) c. Run a traffic control tower
    ( ) d. Mold with clay and putty

11. ( ) a. Analyze your budget
    ( ) b. Study literature
    ( ) c. Visualize and rearrange furniture
    ( ) d. Be an artist

12. ( ) a. Plan a trip and make a budget
    ( ) b. Write a novel
    ( ) c. Build a house or shack
    ( ) d. Make crafts your hobby

Quadrant Analysis

Scoring: Add the number of responses for each of the four categories (a, b, c, and d) and enter them into the quadrants below.

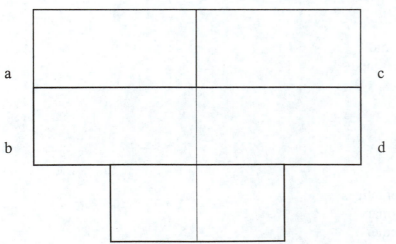

The four cells of the quadrant are (a) Left (Logical); (b) Left (Verbal); (c) Right (Manipulative-Spatial); and (d) Right (Creative). To obtain the left and right scores, add (a) and (b) for Left and (c) and (d) for Right hemispheric preferences. Wagner and Wells note that a difference of *at least* 3 points between L and R is needed to show a significant difference between L and R. Otherwise, the score is considered Balanced.

Wagner and Wells reported some success in predicting the hemispheric preferences of such criterion groups as senior college students in a Logic class [Left, Logic (a)], creative writers [Left, Verbal (b) and Right, Creative (d)], vocational-technical high school teachers [Right, Manipulative (c)], nurses [Right, Manipulative (c)], and visual artists (painters) [Right, Creative (d)]. They were less successful in using the L/R dichotomy in their predictions, and suggested that this division may be too crude. The quadrant analysis, while requiring further research, may provide useful information for vocational guidance.

What are your current academic interests (major)?

What would you consider your academic strengths? Weaknesses?

How might the results of this inventory help you in vocational planning?

Reference

Wagner, R. F., & Wells, K. A. (1985). A refined neurobehavioral inventory of hemispheric preference. *Journal of Clinical Psychology, 41*, 671–676.

Name _____

Date _____

ACTIVE LEARNING EXPERIENCE

2.3   PEDIGREE CHART

Psychologists frequently acknowledge the contributions of heredity and environment to individual differences in behavior. The following activity is designed to illustrate the role of heredity in a common source of human variation—tongue rolling, the ability to roll up the edges of the tongue lengthwise into a U shape.   The roller phenotype is regarded as the dominant trait, consisting of genotypes RR and Rr. Non-rollers are rr. As Jones and Richards (1991) noted, while it is likely an oversimplification, for our purpose we can consider this trait "to exist in only the two forms mentioned and to be determined by a single gene with two alleles, one of which is dominant" (p. 173).

A pedigree chart is a shorthand way of illustrating the history of a genetic trait (e.g., tongue rolling) within a family. Analysis of this chart will help you determine the mode of transmission of tongue rolling in your family.

Construct a pedigree chart on tongue rolling for your family, going back as far as you can. Use the figure below for symbols and designations.

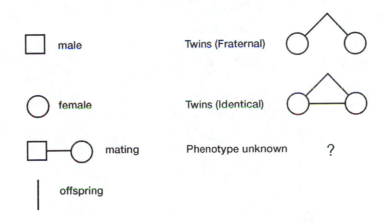

Darken the symbol of any family member who exhibits the trait

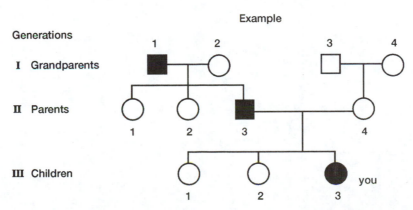

Pedigree Chart

Typically, dominant traits appear at a ratio of 3:1, or 75% of the time, in the general population. Is this true for your pedigree?

From your pedigree, can you tell which individuals in your family are tongue rollers but carry a gene for being a non-roller? Explain.

What are the proportions of tongue-rollers and non-rollers in your class? Do they fit the 3:1 ratio?

Reference

Jones, R. N., & Richards, G. K. (1991). *Practical genetics*. Philadelphia: Open University Press.

CHAPTER 3

SENSATION AND PERCEPTION

Name _____

Date _____

ACTIVE LEARNING EXPERIENCE

3.1 SENSITIVITY

Josh Gerow (1997) described an interesting way to assess sensitivity. It requires some props—250 pennies and two identical, *very light-weight* containers. [I've found that cardboard or styrofoam containers or cups from fast food restaurants work well.] You will also need to recruit a volunteer to serve as your subject.

In this experiment, you will be measuring a *difference threshold*—the smallest difference between stimuli that can be detected 50% of the time. In this *simplified* version of a psychophysiological experiment, you will use the Method of Limits to measure your subject's ability to judge the difference between two weights.

Explain to your subject that you will be presenting him/her with two weights, one right after the other placed in his/her preferred hand. Your subject only has to say whether the weights are the same or different.

Have your subject sit on a chair and blindfold him/her. Present this experiment in two phases.

Task 1

Fill the "standard" container with 50 pennies and the "comparison" container with 70. Present the stimuli in the following sequence, until he/she reports that they are the *same*.

Trial	Standard	Comparison	Response
1	50	70	_____
2	50	69	_____
3	50	68	_____
4	50	67	_____
5	50	66	_____
6	50	65	_____
7	50	64	_____
8	50	63	_____
9	50	62	_____
10	50	61	_____
11	50	60	_____
12	50	59	_____
13	50	58	_____
14	50	57	_____
15	50	56	_____

Trial	Standard	Comparison	Response
16	50	55	_____
17	50	54	_____
18	50	53	_____
19	50	52	_____
20	50	51	_____
21	50	50	_____

NOTE: If on either task your subject reports that the stimuli are the "same" on the first trial *add* rather than subtract from the comparison and continue until he/she reports that they are "different." Once this task is completed, begin the second task.

Task 2

This time fill the "standard" container with 100 pennies and the "comparison" container with 130. Present the stimuli in the following sequence until he/she reports that they are the "same."

Trial	Standard	Comparison	Response
1	100	130	_____
2	100	129	_____
3	100	128	_____
4	100	127	_____
5	100	126	_____
6	100	125	_____
7	100	124	_____
8	100	123	_____
9	100	122	_____
10	100	121	_____
11	100	120	_____
12	100	119	_____
13	100	118	_____
14	100	117	_____
15	100	116	_____
16	100	115	_____
17	100	114	_____
18	100	113	_____
19	100	112	_____
20	100	111	_____
21	100	110	_____
22	100	109	_____
23	100	108	_____
24	100	107	_____
25	100	106	_____
26	100	105	_____
27	100	104	_____
28	100	103	_____
29	100	102	_____
30	100	101	_____
31	100	100	_____

Although a typical psychophysiological experiment would require many series of descending and ascending trials to accurately determine a subject's difference threshold, this experiment should give you an idea of what the process is like. It may also demonstrate some basic psychophysiological principles.

What was the just noticeable difference (JND)—or the smallest difference between the two stimuli where the subject is able to detect a difference (i.e., the last trial before the subject reports that they are the same)—for each task?

task 1 _____

task 2 _____

Do you notice a relationship between the JND's for each task? If so, what is it?

You probably found that the JND for task 2 was larger than for task 1. Psychophysiologists are concerned with this relationship between the intensity of physical stimuli and the subject's psychological reaction. Ernest Weber, in the 1800s, reported that the absolute size of the change was not that important but the relative size of the change was important in determining the subject's psychological reaction. In this experiment, your subject's JND in the second task should be approximately twice as much as in the first task because the intensity of the stimulus in task 2 was twice as great as it was in task 1. Although Weber's law does not hold for high or low intensity stimuli, it is a useful theory for a large range of stimuli.

Reference

Gerow, J. R. (1997). *Psychology: An introduction* (5th ed.). New York: Longman.

Name _____

Date _____

ACTIVE LEARNING EXPERIENCE

3.2   PERCEPTION

If you were asked to describe the figure below, how would you describe it?

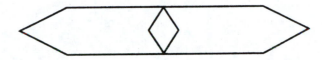

Description:

How would you describe this figure?

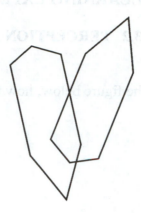

Description:

In both cases, most people describe two figures, but the descriptions differ considerably. The reason the descriptions differ is that perception is governed by organizing principles (Nearness, Similarity, Continuation, Closure, and Fate) from Gestalt Psychology.

The principle that influences perception of these two figures is "good continuation." It seems to work automatically and most people do not realize that the two figures are made of the same elements. Look at each of the two figures closely and see if you can identify the two identical components of each.

Identify other situations you experienced where the Gestalt principles of perception operate.

Reference

Figures adapted from Wertheimer, M. (1923). Studies in the theory of Gestalt psychology. *Psychologische Forschung, 4*, 301–350.

Name _____

Date _____

ACTIVE LEARNING EXPERIENCE

3.3 STROOP EFFECT

J. R. Stroop (1935), in a classic experiment, demonstrated the role of attention in perception. Below is an adaptation of his experiment. You will need a stopwatch and a volunteer to serve as your subject.

Tell your subject that when you say "begin," he/she is to name the pictures as quickly as possible. [Use the list of correct answers to check for accuracy as your subject progresses through the list.]

Say—Ready? Begin (as you turn the page and start the stopwatch).

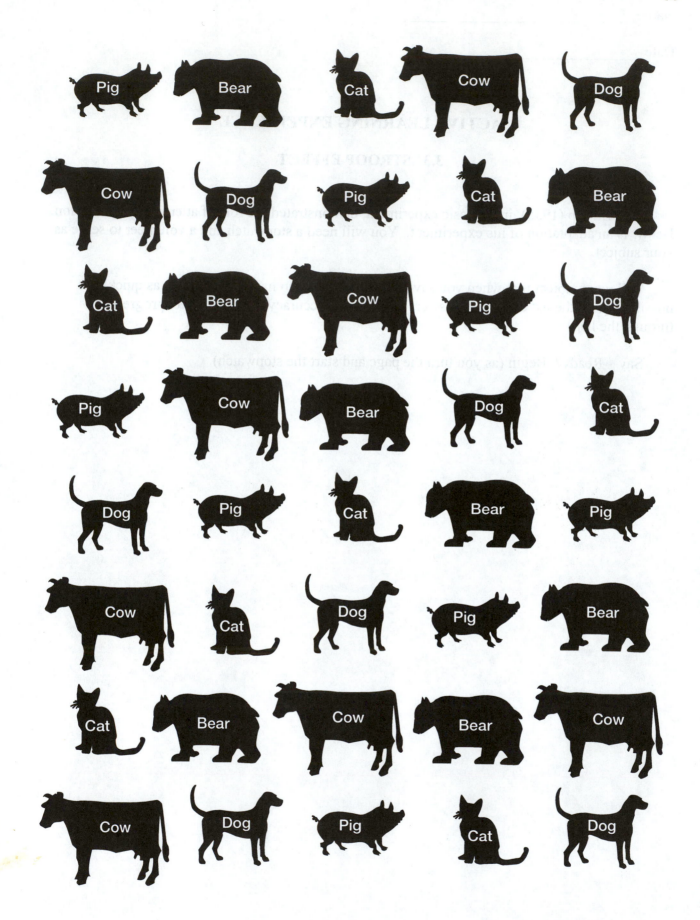

Now, follow the same procedure for the second set of items. [Use the list of correct answers to check for accuracy as your subject progresses through the list.]

ANSWER SHEET

List 1

1. Pig	9. Bear	17. Cat	25. Cow	33. Dog
2. Cow	10. Dog	18. Pig	26. Cat	34. Bear
3. Cat	11. Bear	19. Cow	27. Pig	35. Dog
4. Pig	12. Cow	20. Bear	28. Dog	36. Cat
5. Dog	13. Pig	21. Cat	29. Bear	37. Pig
6. Cow	14. Cat	22. Dog	30. Pig	38. Bear
7. Cat	15. Bear	23. Cow	31. Bear	39. Cow
8. Cow	16. Dog	24. Pig	32. Cat	40. Dog

List 2

1. Dog	9. Cow	17. Bear	25. Pig	33. Cat
2. Pig	10. Bear	18. Cow	26. Cat	34. Dog
3. Bear	11. Pig	19. Dog	27. Bear	35. Pig
4. Cow	12. Cat	20. Pig	28. Cow	36. Dog
5. Dog	13. Cow	21. Cat	29. Pig	37. Cow
6. Bear	14. Dog	22. Cow	30. Cat	38. Pig
7. Pig	15. Bear	23. Dog	31. Bear	39. Cat
8. Cat	16. Dog	24. Cat	32. Cow	40. Bear

Set 1

    Time _____   Errors _____

Set 2

    Time _____   Errors _____

Did you notice any differences in times and/or errors for the two sets? Was one more difficult than the other? Why? (Ask your subject to comment about the relative difficulty of the two sets.)

Are there any other circumstances that you can think of that might affect performance? How?

This experiment emphasizes the role of attention in processing information. In both sets 1 and 2, two pathways are activated (picture and word). When they are compatible (e.g., the word cow and picture of cow), they should facilitate performance. When they are incompatible (as in set 2), interference occurs and disrupts performance.

Reference

Stroop, J. R. (1935). Studies of interference in serial verbal reactions. *Journal of Experimental Psychology, 18,* 643–662.

CHAPTER 4

CONSCIOUSNESS

Name _____

Date _____

ACTIVE LEARNING EXPERIENCE

4.1   CIRCADIAN RHYTHMS

Circadian rhythms are biological changes that occur during each 24-hour day. They not only affect our sleep and waking cycles, but also such processes as blood pressure, pulse rate, body temperature, and blood-sugar level.

To assess your own rhythms, answer the following questions designed by J. A. Horne and O. Östberg (1976).

Instructions:
1. Please read each question very carefully before answering.
2. Answer ALL questions.
3. Answer questions in numerical order.
4. Each question should be answered independently of others. Do NOT go back and check your answers.
5. All questions have a selection of answers. For each question place a cross alongside ONE answer only. Some questions have a scale instead of a selection of answers. Place a cross at the appropriate point along the scale.

1. Considering only your own "feeling best" rhythm, at what time would you get up if you were entirely free to plan your day?

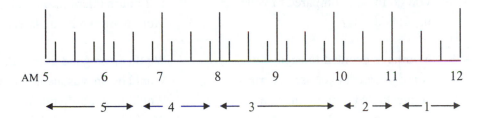

2. Considering only your own "feeling best" rhythm, at what time would you go to bed if you were entirely free to plan your evening?

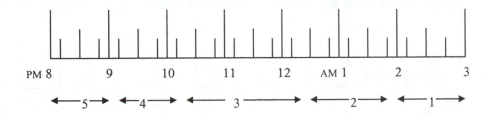

3. If there is a specific time at which you have to get up in the morning, to what extent are you dependent on being woken up by an alarm clock?

Not at all dependent	☐	4
Slightly dependent	☐	3
Fairly dependent	☐	2
Very dependent	☐	1

4. Assuming adequate environmental conditions, how easy do you find getting up in the morning?

Not at all easy	☐	1
Not very easy	☐	2
Fairly easy	☐	3
Very easy	☐	4

5. How alert do you feel during the first half hour after having woken in the morning?

Not at all alert	☐	1
Slightly alert	☐	2
Fairly alert	☐	3
Very alert	☐	4

6. How is your appetite during the first half-hour after having woken in the morning?

Very poor	☐	1
Fairly poor	☐	2
Fairly good	☐	3
Very good	☐	4

7. During the first half-hour after having woken in the morning, how tired do you feel?

Very tired	☐	1
Fairy tired	☐	2
Fairly refreshed	☐	3
Very refreshed	☐	4

8. When you have no commitments the next day, at what time do you go to bed compared to your usual bedtime?

Seldom or never later	☐	4
Less than one hour later	☐	3
1–2 hours later	☐	2
More than two hours later	☐	1

9. You have decided to engage in some physical exercise. A friend suggests that you do this one hour twice a week and the best time for him is between 7:00–8:00 AM. Bearing in mind nothing else but your own "feeling best" rhythm How do you think you would perform?

Would be on good form	☐	4
Would be on reasonable form	☐	3
Would find it difficult	☐	2
Would find it very difficult	☐	1

10. At what time in the evening do you feel tired and as a result in need of sleep?

| PM 8 | 9 | 10 | 11 | 12 | AM 1 | 2 | 3 |

←—5—→   ←—4—→   ←———3———→   ←—2—→   ←—1—→

11. You wish to be at your peak performance for a test which you know is going to be mentally exhausting and lasting for two hours. You are entirely free to plan your day and considering only your own "feeling best" rhythm which ONE of the four testing times would you choose?

8:00–10:00 AM...............	☐	6
11:00 AM–1:00 PM.........	☐	4
3:00–5:00 PM...............	☐	2
7:00–9:00 PM...............	☐	0

12. If you went to bed at 11:00 PM at what level of tiredness would you be?

Not at all tired	☐	0
A little tired	☐	2
Fairly tired	☐	3
Very tired	☐	5

13. For some reason you have gone to bed several hours later than usual, but there is no need to get up at any particular time the next morning. Which ONE of the following events are you most likely to experience?

Will wake up at usual time and will NOT fall asleep	☐	4
Will wake up at usual time and will doze thereafter	☐	3
Will wake up at usual time but will fall asleep again	☐	2
Will NOT wake up until later than usual	☐	1

14. One night you have to remain awake between 4:00–6:00 AM in order to carry out a night watch. You have no commitments the next day. Which ONE of the following alternatives will suit you best?

Would NOT go to bed until watch was over	☐	1
Would take a nap before and sleep after	☐	2
Would take a good sleep before and nap after	☐	3
Would take ALL sleep before watch	☐	4

15. You have to do two hours of hard physical work. You are entirely free to plan your day and considering only your own "feeling best" rhythm which ONE of the following times would you choose?

8:00–10:00 AM	☐	4
11:00–1:00 AM	☐	3
3:00–5:00 PM	☐	2
7:00–9:00 PM	☐	1

16. You have decided to engage in hard physical exercise. A friend suggests that you do this for one hour twice a week and the best time for him is between 10:00–11:00 PM. Bearing in mind nothing else but your own "feeling best" rhythm how well do you think you would perform?

Would be on good form	☐	1
Would be on reasonable form	☐	2
Would find it difficult	☐	3
Would find it very difficult	☐	4

17. Suppose that you can choose your own work hours. Assume that you worked a FIVE hour day (including breaks) and that your job was interesting and paid by results. Which FIVE CONSECUTIVE hours would you select?

```
☐☐☐☐☐☐☐☐☐☐☐☐☐☐☐☐☐☐☐☐☐☐☐☐
```
12 1 2 3 4 5 6 7 8 9 10 11 12 1 2 3 4 5 6 7 8 9 10 11 12
MIDNIGHT   NOON   MIDNIGHT

←------- 1 --→ ←------ 5 ---→ ← 4→ ←---3 ------→ ←--- 2 → ←----------- 1 ----------------→

18. At what time of the day do you think that you reach your "feeling best" peak?

```
☐☐☐☐☐☐☐☐☐☐☐☐☐☐☐☐☐☐☐☐☐☐☐☐
```
12 1 2 3 4 5 6 7 8 9 10 11 12 1 2 3 4 5 6 7 8 9 10 11 12
MIDNIGHT   NOON   MIDNIGHT

←------- 1 --------→ ←- 5 ---→ ← 4 → ←-----------3 -------------→ ←--- 2 ----------------→ ←--- 1 -→

19. One hears about "morning" and "evening" types of people.
Which ONE of these types do you consider yourself to be?

Definitely a "morning" type	☐	6
Rather more a "morning" than an "evening" type	☐	4
Rather more an "evening" than a "morning" type	☐	2
Definitely an "evening" type	☐	0

Scoring. For questions 3, 4, 5, 6, 7, 8, 9, 11, 12, 13, 14, 15, 16, and 19, the appropriate score for each response is displayed beside the answer box.

For questions 1, 2, 10, and 18, the appropriate score is displayd below the answer box. For question 17 the most extreme cross on the right hand side is taken as the reference point and the appropriate score below this point is taken.

The scores are added together and the sum converted into a five point Morningness-Eveningness score: [Score = _____]

Interpretation

	Score
Definitely Morning Type	70–86
Moderately Morning Type	59–69
Neither Type	42–58
Moderately Evening Type	31–41
Definitely Evening Type	16–30

How does your cycle influence your behavior in the following areas:

Your personal life:

Your social life:

Academics:

Employment:

How can you adjust your life to better conform to your "peak" periods?

Reference

From Horne, J. A., & Östberg, O. (1976). A self-assessment questionnaire to determine morningness-eveningness in human circadian rhythms. *International Journal of Chronobiology, 4,* 97–110. Reprinted with permission of Gordon and Breach Publishers.

Name _____

Date _____

ACTIVE LEARNING EXPERIENCE

4.2 DAYDREAM RECORDING AND ANALYSIS

Daydreaming is an altered state of consciousness that most people are familiar with but few fully understand. However, as Jerome Singer and Ellen Switzer (1980) noted, fantasy, daydreams, and related activities (e.g., imagery) can serve many valuable purposes, including effective planning for the future, enhancing creativity, controlling undesirable habits, and increasing sexual pleasure. It is also believed that our daydreams provide links to our psychological makeup. And, by analyzing our daydreams, we can gain insight into our needs, motives, and concerns.

For each of the next three days, jot down your daydreams, being as detailed as possible. Rather than carry this book around, you might want to carry a pocket-size notebook or 3 x 5 cards and transfer the information here at the end of each day.

Day 1

Day 2

Day 3

While an examination of *content* of daydreams (especially if there are recurring themes) may provide valuable insights about specific concerns, Eric Klinger (1990) pointed out that daydream *patterns* could be reduced to three psychological styles:

1. positive-constructive (vivid, upbeat, constructive, enjoyable daydreams)
2. guilty-fearful (unpleasant daydreams dealing with guilt, depression, fear)
3. poor attentional control (attention jumps from one thing to the next)

How would you classify your daydream patterns? And how would you account for this classification?

Klinger further noted that if your daydreams are predominantly in the *positive-constructive* category "you take real delight in many of your daydreams, you tend to experience them as vivid mental pictures and sounds and you get deeply absorbed in them" (p. 99). You likely have more daydreams than the average and they are productive in helping you to solve problems.

If your daydreams are predominantly in the *guilty-fearful* category "many of your daydreams have a negative cast" (p. 99). "They reflect your fears, your regrets, and the things you feel guilty about. People who have many unpleasant daydreams often daydream about failing, doing something embarrassing, or feeling afraid and guilty" (p. 104).

If your daydreams are predominantly in the poor attentional control category, you have "a high degree of inner distraction, have trouble concentrating, and become easily bored" (p. 99). "People who have trouble focusing their thoughts also tend to have less focused lives" (p. 105). "[T]hey tend to feel less in control of their lives—as if what they do for themselves may be less important than the lucky breaks or disasters imposed on them by other people or by fate" (p. 105).

If you fall into one of the latter two categories, don't despair. You have just taken an important step toward change—identifying the problem.

Most of us are more aware of our overt behavior than our thoughts, but our thoughts go a long way toward determining how we feel and behave. Cognitive psychologists stress the importance of productive thinking in enriching our lives. Techniques ranging from self-talk to guided imagery can facilitate this process. In essence, by positively restructuring our inner experiences, such as daydreaming, our overt behavior can also change. You will read more about cognitive approaches to change later in the course.

References

Klinger, E. (1990). *Daydreaming*. Los Angeles: Tarcher.

Singer, J. L., & Suitzer, E. (1980). *Mind play: The creative uses of fantasy*. Englewood Cliffs, NJ: Prentice-Hall.

Name _____

Date _____

ACTIVE LEARNING EXPERIENCE

4.3 MEDITATION

Meditation has gained popularity in recent years because it is believed to be effective in reducing stress and altering significant biological processes (e.g., lowering blood pressure). The goal of meditation is to establish a state of deep relaxation. By narrowing concentration to one repetitive stimulus, you should be able to block out other stimuli.

One way to accomplish this state is through concentration on slow, deep diaphragmatic breathing. Set aside about 20 minutes each day for the next week to perform the following activity.

Find a room where you will be free of distraction and interruptions. Sit in a comfortable position with the lights dimmed or off. Close your eyes, sit quietly, clear your mind of everything except your breathing—long, deep breaths preferably through your nostrils to your abdomen. Place your right hand on your abdomen with your little finger just above your belly button and your left hand on your chest. Proper breathing will move your right hand noticeably, but not your left.

Spend at least 10 minutes the first day and try to work up to 20 minutes.

Describe your mental and physical states after each session:

1.

2.

3.

4.

5.

6.

7.

Did you notice any changes over time? If so, what were they? If not, did you have any difficulties with the activity? If so, what were they?

CHAPTER 5

LEARNING

Name _____

Date _____

ACTIVE LEARNING EXPERIENCE

5.1 OPERANT CONDITIONING

Reinforcement, especially social reinforcement, is important to most of us. It is not surprising, then, that social reinforcement, even when subtly applied, exerts a powerful influence on our behavior. To examine the role of social reinforcement in an operant conditioning paradigm, try the following adaptation of Greenspoon's (1955) classic "plural nouns" verbal conditioning procedure.

You will need a stopwatch and a volunteer to serve as a subject.

Both you and your subject should be seated about five feet apart in comfortable chairs facing each other. Instruct the subject to simply say words, all the words that he/she can think of without using sentences or phrases, or counting. Tell the subject not to go too rapidly because you are taking notes.

Following every *plural noun* uttered, immediately nod your head and say "Mm-hmm" or "good." Do not respond verbally or nonverbally to any other words. Keep track of the number of plural nouns uttered during each three minute interval by simply making a check mark for each one. Be careful to shield your tally sheet from your subject so he/she will not see what you are doing.

First 3 minutes

Total _____

Second 3 minutes

Total _____

Third 3 minutes

Total _____

Fourth 3 minutes

Total _____

Fifth 3 minutes

Total _____

Describe your results across the five intervals.

How would you interpret the results? Was the conditioning procedure successful in increasing the rate of plural nouns from the first to the fifth interval? If not, what factors do you think might account for the failure?

Reference

Greenspoon, J. (1955). The reinforcing effect of two spoken sounds on the frequency of two responses. *American Journal of Psychology, 68,* 409–416.

Name _____

Date _____

ACTIVE LEARNING EXPERIENCE

5.2 CLASSICAL CONDITIONING

Paul Rozin, Linda Millman, and Carol Nemeroff (1986) conducted an interesting series of experiments that help us to understand our taste preferences. Below is an adapted version of their work.

Using a scale from -10 (most unpleasant experience you can imagine) through 0 (neutral experience) to +10 (most pleasant experience you can imagine), rate the following experiences.

	Rating
Imagine a bowl of your favorite soup.	_____
Imagine your favorite soup served in a brand-new bedpan.	_____
Imagine a piece of your favorite candy.	_____
Imagine a piece of your favorite candy shaped in the form of a rat.	_____
Imagine your favorite pizza.	_____
Imagine your favorite pizza served to you on a brand-new fly swatter.	_____
Imagine your favorite mixed drink.	_____
Imagine your favorite mixed drink stirred with a brand-new comb.	_____

If you experienced less pleasant reactions to the second alternative of any of these four pairings, you are exhibiting a classically conditioned reaction. As Rozin and his associates noted, "The associations of negative items with objects can lead, by a process of evaluative conditioning, to devaluation of the objects" (p. 710).

You may have experienced similar occurrences in your own life. Here's one of mine. My friend Tracey refused to drink a glass of water I poured her from a pitcher shaped like a rooster, because it looked to her like the rooster was "barfing" into her glass! In this case, the negative image of the rooster barfing was associated with the water and resulted in an aversive reaction.

List an example of a classically conditioned aversive reaction of your own:

Reference

Rozin, P., Millman, L., & Nemeroff, C. (1986). Operation of the laws of sympathetic magic in disgust and other domains. *Journal of Personality and Social Psychology, 50,* 703–712.

Name _____

Date _____

ACTIVE LEARNING EXPERIENCE

5.3 COGNITIVE MAP

When I first read a review of Edward Tolman's (1948) research on latent learning and cognitive maps, the following event came to mind:

> "My first day of school was memorable. With tears streaming down my face and accompanied by my mother, I passed through busy city streets on the half-mile walk to school. The volume and intensity of my cries increased as we entered the school and peaked when my mother left. I did not want to stay there, especially without my mother! Eventually, though, I stopped crying and started planning. The first chance I would get, I was out of there. My opportunity came during recess, and I quietly slipped away. When I announced my arrival home, my mother, who was hanging laundry on the back porch, screamed and nearly fell over the railing. She was not as pleased to see me as I had imagined." (Brannigan, 1996, pp. 263–264)

It is likely that I had developed a cognitive representation of my environment that allowed me to easily navigate through a busy city at four and one-half years of age. Tolman believed that not all learning was of the stimulus-response variety. Rather, we continually gather information, even in the absence of reinforcement and any thoughts about how or when that information might be used. The information we gather allows us to form cognitive maps that influence many aspects of our lives, from simple travel around a home-town neighborhood to complex decision making on ethical and moral issues. To better understand how cognitive maps influence your behavior, Alan Swinkels and Traci Giuliano (1997) suggest a simple demonstration that involves a cognitive map of a familiar place, such as your college campus. Visualize the campus and draw it (use pencil) with as much detail as possible. It might surprise you to see how much you know!

Map

What did you discover about your knowledge of your campus from this experience?

Tolman noted that the broader and more comprehensive our maps, the greater our adaptability. Consider your cognitive map of your campus. Although you will continue to add information to the map with further experience, it is much more efficient now than when you first arrived on campus. You can likely get from point A to point B relatively easily by referring to your cognitive map (even if you have never actually made this particular trip before). In contrast, your first day on campus may have been a study in frustration even if you were *given* a campus map.

What do you find in comparing your map with those of other students (especially those who have been there longer), or comparing students who live on campus with commuting students?

Tolman encouraged the development of broad, comprehensive cognitive maps in all aspects of our lives. The knowledge we gain helps us to become better people in "that great . . . maze which is our human world" (1948, p. 208).

References

Brannigan, G. G. (1996). What can a "squiggles" test tell us about children? In G. G. Brannigan (Ed.). *The enlightened educator: Research adventures in the schools* (pp. 262–279). New York: McGraw-Hill.

Swinkels, A., & Giuliano, T. (1997). Instructor's resource manual for *Psychology* by S. E. Davis & J. J. Paladino (2nd Ed.). Upper Saddle River, NJ: Prentice-Hall.

Tolman, E. C. (1948). Cognitive maps in rats and men. *Psychological Review, 55,* 189–208.

CHAPTER 6

MEMORY

Name _____

Date _____

ACTIVE LEARNING EXPERIENCE

6.1 MEMORY PHENOMENA

One of the most effective ways to learn about the principles of memory is to draw on your own experience. This activity is based on an elaborate research study by Glenn Meyer and Kathie Hilterbrand (1984).

In the spaces below, write down the names of the Seven Dwarfs from the Walt Disney film *Snow White and the Seven Dwarfs*. Fill all *seven* spaces, even if you have to guess.

_____

_____

_____

_____

_____

_____

_____

Before checking your answers or reading further, respond to the following five questions.

1.   Did you find this task difficult? Why or why not?

2.   Which names were easier to remember? Speculate why.

3.   Which names were harder to remember? Speculate why.

4.   Did you use any strategies or techniques to try to recall any of the names? If so, describe them.

5. Examine the following list of names. Circle the correct names of the Seven Dwarfs. (Do not circle more than or fewer than seven.)

1. Grouchy	8. Jumpy	15. Shorty	22. Wishful
2. Smiley	9. Sniffy	16. Nifty	23. Cheerful
3. Droopy	10. Grumpy	17. Happy	24. Shy
4. Sleepy	11. Puffy	18. Wheezy	25. Bashful
5. Dumpy	12. Lazy	19. Fearful	26. Pop
6. Gabby	13. Sneezy	20. Doc	27. Teach
7. Dopey	14. Stubby	21. Hopeful	

Before going on to the next page, check your results on both tasks. The names of the Seven Dwarfs are in the following positions in the list: Numbers 4, 7, 10, 13, 17, 20, and 25.

Compare your performance on the second task to the first task.

Marianne Miserandino (1991) added an interesting component to this activity that you can try if you were unsuccessful in naming the Seven Dwarfs on either or both of the previous two tasks.

Without looking back, name the Seven Dwarfs:

_____

_____

_____

_____

_____

_____

_____

Check back and see how you did.

The first task is a recall task. The second task, which is generally easier, involves recognition, and suggests that we had more information stored than we were able to recall. The third task involves some learning, unless you had perfect performance earlier.

Meyer and Hilterbrand found that only 22 of 141 college subjects (16%) correctly recalled all seven dwarfs. The average percentage of correct responses was 69%. Recognition performance was much better than recall. The average percentage of correct responses was 86%.

Sleepy (83%) was recalled most frequently, followed by Dopey (81%), Grumpy (77%), Sneezy (76%), Happy (62%), Doc (57%), and Bashful (35%). The position in which they were recalled also closely followed this pattern. Recognition for each of the individual dwarfs was also high (at least 70%).

How did your performance on the various tasks compare with Meyer and Hilterbrand's subjects? Explain why.

Recall:

Recognition:

References

Meyer, G. E., & Hilterbrand, K. (1984). Does it pay to be "bashful"? The seven dwarfs and long term memory. *American Journal of Psychology, 97*, 47–55.

Miserandino, M. (1991). Memory and the seven dwarfs. *Teaching of Psychology, 18*, 169–171.

Name _____

Date _____

ACTIVE LEARNING EXPERIENCE

6.2 POLLYANNA PRINCIPLE

Margaret Matlin, David Stang, Valerie Gawron, Alan Freedman, and Paul Derby (1979) conducted a series of experiments that help to shed light on information processing and memory. The activity below is a slight adaptation of this research based on Matlin's (1999) guidelines.

List ten *colors* in the spaces below:

_____

_____

_____

_____

_____

_____

_____

_____

_____

_____

List ten *vegetables* in the spaces below:

_____

_____

_____

_____

_____

_____

_____

_____

_____

List ten *former teachers* in the spaces below:

_____

_____

_____

_____

_____

_____

_____

_____

_____

_____

In the spaces below, arrange your lists in alphabetical order:

Colors	**Vegetables**	**Teachers**
_____	_____	_____
_____	_____	_____
_____	_____	_____
_____	_____	_____
_____	_____	_____
_____	_____	_____
_____	_____	_____
_____	_____	_____
_____	_____	_____
_____	_____	_____

Separately, for *each* list, rank order each member with respect to the other members on the list on a "one" (favorite) to "ten" (least favorite) scale.

Then, transfer the rankings to your original lists.

In examining your original lists (especially comparing the first and last members of each list), do you detect any pattern or trend? If so, what is it and what do you think it means for memory?

Most people recall more pleasant memories first. Matlin and her associates (1979) described this as a selectivity phenomenon that affects information processing from input to output where "pleasant information is processed more effectively and more accurately than less pleasant information" (p. 10). This has been termed the "Pollyanna Principle." How might this information affect other aspects of your life?

References

Matlin, M. W. (1999). *Cognition* (4th ed.). Fort Worth, TX: Harcourt.

Matlin, M. W., Stang, D. J., Gawron V. J., Freedman, A., & Derby, P. L. (1979). Evaluative measuring as a determinant of spew positions. *The Journal of General Psychology, 100*, 3–11.

Name _____

Date _____

ACTIVE LEARNING EXPERIENCE

6.3 MEMORY STRATEGIES

Gordon Bower and David Winzenz (1970) conducted an interesting experiment to compare the effectiveness of different learning strategies. The following activity is an adaptation of their experiment. Before proceeding, cover List 1. You will need a stopwatch and someone to keep time for you.

Learn the following list of pairs by simply REPEATING the members of each pair. Using **only** this learning strategy, go through the list as many times as you can in 75 seconds.

Ready? Begin.

List 1

1. Horse - Table
2. Island - Hat
3. Door - Note
4. Bear-Apple
5. Clock-Moon
6. Building - Dog
7. River - Table
8. Road - Paper
9. Basket - Cloud
10. Ring - Ship
11. Snow - Window
12. Pencil - Hammer
13. Bread - Car
14. Meat - Envelope
15. Box - Garden

When you finish, go immediately to the next page.

Try to recall as many of the pairs as you can.

Snow - _____   Ring - _____

Bear - _____   Clock - _____

Road - _____   Door - _____

Basket - _____   Meat - _____

Horse - _____   River - _____

Box - _____   Pencil - _____

Island - _____   Building - _____

Bread - _____

How many pairs did you recall correctly? _____

How effective was this strategy?

When you are ready to continue this activity, have a piece of paper ready to cover List 2 on the next page.

Cover List 2.

Now, try a different strategy on the following list of pairs. For each pair, "visualize a mental picture or image in which the two [members] are in some kind of vivid interaction. . . . make [the] image as elaborate, vivid, or bizarre as [you] wish" (p. 119). The key is to SEE IT! For example, if the pair is SHOE - SPAGHETTI you could picture a shoe with spaghetti for laces. You have 75 seconds to spend on this list.

Ready? Begin.

List 2

1. Bird - Fruit
2. Rain - Rock
3. Dress - Money
4. House - Mountain
5. Cow - Flower
6. Corn - Gate
7. Roof - Nest
8. Baby - Hair
9. Ice - Train
10. Fence - Letter
11. Egg - Chair
12. Book - Water
13. Coat - Glass
14. Candy - Sign
15. Rabbit - Paint

When you finish, go immediately to the next page.

Try to recall as many of the pairs as you can.

Book - _____   Bird - _____

House - _____   Coat - _____

Rabbit - _____   Corn - _____

Rain - _____   Egg - _____

Ice - _____   Candy - _____

Baby - _____   Cow - _____

Fence - _____   Roof - _____

Dress - _____

How many pairs did you recall correctly? _____

How effective was this strategy in comparison to the first strategy?

If there was a difference in the two strategies, what do you think accounted for the difference?

If you are like most people, you performed noticeably better on the second task than the first. Gordon and Winzenz (1970) found that the visualization technique greatly improved recall over the rote repetition technique (approximately 13 words to 6 words recalled!). Can you apply this technique to learning and remembering information in this course? Give an example.

Reference

Bower, G. H., & Winzenz, D. (1970). Comparison of associative learning strategies. *Psychonomic Science, 20,* 119–120.

CHAPTER 7

LANGUAGE, THINKING,

AND INTELLIGENCE

Name _____

Date _____

ACTIVE LEARNING EXPERIENCE

7.1 PUZZLE

At one time or another, you have likely encountered problems that ask you to predict the next number in a sequence. Using the "think aloud" procedure, write down your thoughts about possible solutions as you try them. When you solve the problem or exhaust all your solutions, turn to the next page.

What is the next number in this sequence?

8   5   9   1   7   2   _____

Thoughts:

If your attempts to solve this problem were numerically based, then you have fallen into a common trap. Mental sets, or tendencies to approach problems in certain ways based on our previous experiences, may work against us in problem-solving situations. Your mental set was that the numbers were in some logical *numerical* sequence.

As you struggled with the problem, did any other possible sequence—like a language-based one—cross your mind? Try again, this time exploring language-based solutions. Write down your thoughts as you explore solutions. When you solve the problem or exhaust all your solutions, turn to the next page.

8   5   9   1   7   2   _____

Thoughts:

Hopefully you were successful with the shift from the number to the language-based set. If not, you should expand the language-based possibilities to include an alphabetically based set. Try again. When you solve the problem or exhaust all your solutions, turn to the next page.

Eight five nine one seven two _____

Thoughts:

As you may or may not have detected, the puzzle follows an ascending alphabetical progression from "E" to "T." The next number in the sequence is "zero."

Now that you are aware of the obstacles mental sets present, you should try to expand, rather than limit, your approach to problems. How can you counteract their effects in other aspects of your life?

Name _____

Date _____

ACTIVE LEARNING EXPERIENCE

7.2 CREATIVITY

Divergent thinking is thought to be an important aspect of creativity. It is characterized primarily by fluency, flexibility, and originality of thought. Fluency refers to the number of ideas we generate in a given situation. Flexibility refers to the number of different categories of ideas. And originality refers to the novelty of the ideas. Creative thinkers may be characterized by the fact that they generate a lot of different ideas that are novel.

To assess your capacity for divergent thought, try the following test. In this test, which is an adaptation of an alternative uses test, you will be given some common objects and their typical use. For each object, list up to six other uses that differ from the typical use and from one another. For example, for a Coffee Mug, typically used for drinking, you might list:

1. a planter
2. a pencil holder
3. a cookie cutter
4. to dye Easter eggs
5. to catch dripping water
6. a paper weight

All you will need is a pencil, a stopwatch, and someone to time you. Before turning the page, read the following instructions.

Instructions: On the following page are three objects. List up to six alternate uses for each. You will have four minutes to complete the entire list. When you are ready, turn the page, start the stopwatch, and begin.

A. Book - (to read)

    1. _____

    2. _____

    3. _____

    4. _____

    5. _____

    6. _____

B. Bed Sheet - (to cover a bed)

    1. _____

    2. _____

    3. _____

    4. _____

    5. _____

    6. _____

C. Wire Clothes Hanger - (to hang clothes)

    1. _____

    2. _____

    3. _____

    4. _____

    5. _____

    6. _____

You can compare your performance to your classmates' performance by generating a class mean for fluency/flexibility—the number of *different* ideas (range = 0–18). I have found an average of 12 for college students. Highly creative students generally list 18 alternatives well within the time limits.

You can also compare your *specific* answers with those of your classmates to determine how original they are. Original ideas are those that are appropriate and occur 5% of the time or less.

How did you do in these comparisons?

Would you consider yourself creative? If so, in what ways?

Name _____

Date _____

ACTIVE LEARNING EXPERIENCE

7.3 LANGUAGE AND CONTEXT

Robert Sternberg and Janet Powell (1983) reported on the cognitive basis of verbal comprehension, emphasizing the importance of learning from context. To demonstrate this phenomenon, they used the following procedure:

Can you define the following?

       ceilidh -

       oam -

If not, read the following passage:

> Two ill-dressed people—the one a tired woman of middle years and the other a tense young man—sat around a fire where the common meal was almost ready. The mother, Tanith, peered at her son through the *oam* of the bubbling stew. It had been a long time since his last *ceilidh* and Tobar had changed greatly; where once he had seemed all legs and clumsy joints, he now was well-formed and in control of his hard, young body. As they ate, Tobar told of his past year, recreating for Tanith how he had wandered long and far in his quest to gain the skills he would need to be permitted to rejoin the company. Then all too soon, their brief *ceilidh* over, Tobar walked over to touch his mother's arm and quickly left. (p. 884)

Can you make a better attempt at defining the following?

ceilidh -

oam -

Sternberg and Powell described eight kinds of information about unknown words that we can glean from the context. They include cues about time, location, value, physical properties, functions, causation, class membership, and meaning. What were some of the clues that helped you with ceilidh?

What were some of the clues that helped you with oam?

Reference

Sternberg, R. J., & Powell, J. S. (1983). Comprehending verbal comprehension. *American Psychologist, 38*, 878–893.

CHAPTER 8

MOTIVATION AND EMOTION

Name _____

Date _____

ACTIVE LEARNING EXPERIENCE

8.1 MOTIVES

The following activity, developed by Anthony Grasha (1995), will give you an idea of how Abraham Maslow's Need Hierarchy applies to your life.

Psychologist Abraham Maslow (1970) suggested that our motives can be organized into a hierarchy, with basic survival and safety needs at the bottom and social, self-esteem, and self-actualization (i.e., our attempts to achieve our potential in life) on the upper levels of this hierarchy. This activity is designed to help you explore some of the implications of Maslow's thinking in your life.

PART 1

Think about the activities you engaged in during the past two to three weeks. Next, review the list of needs presented below, and place a check next to those you remember trying to satisfy. Then, concentrate on one or more examples of how you tried to satisfy that need, and rate how satisfied you were satisfying that need.

1	2	3	4	5
Very Dissatisfied	**Moderately Dissatisfied**	**Neutral**	**Moderately Satisfied**	**Very Satisfied**

Maslow's Need Hierarchy	**Tried to Satisfy**	**Satisfaction Rating**
Physiological		
Hunger	_____	_____
Thirst	_____	_____
Sex	_____	_____
Sleep	_____	_____
Rest	_____	_____
Exercise	_____	_____
Safety		
Shelter	_____	_____
Protection	_____	_____
Physical	_____	_____
Psychological	_____	_____
Economic	_____	_____

1	2	3	4	5
Very Dissatisfied	**Moderately Dissatisfied**	**Neutral**	**Moderately Satisfied**	**Very Satisfied**

Maslow's Need Hierarchy	**Tried to Satisfy**	**Satisfaction Rating**
Social		
Displaying love and affection	_____	_____
Seeking friendships	_____	_____
Affiliating with others	_____	_____
Self-esteem		
Developing confidence	_____	_____
Seeking independence	_____	_____
Achieving something	_____	_____
Obtaining influence	_____	_____
Obtaining knowledge	_____	_____
Gaining recognition	_____	_____
Obtaining status	_____	_____
Seeking respect	_____	_____
Self-actualization		
Trying to achieve your potential	_____	_____
Engaging in self-development	_____	_____
Behaving creatively	_____	_____
Displaying an acceptance of self	_____	_____
Displaying an acceptance of others	_____	_____

PART 2

Pick one or two needs that received the lowest satisfaction ratings, and develop an action plan to increase your ability to satisfy them in the future. Similarly, pick one or two needs you did not check that you would like to spend time working on in the future. What are several specific actions you must take?

Action Plan: Low-Rated Needs

Action Plan: Needs Not Rated but of Interest for Future

PART 3

Maslow suggested that people are more satisfied with their attempts to meet needs lower in the hierarchy than those that were higher. Do your ratings suggest this was true for you?
Yes _____   No _____. Give a brief reason for your response.

Abraham Maslow also noted that people tend not to pursue higher-order needs (i.e., social, self-esteem, self-actualization) unless they were able to satisfy their physiological and safety needs. Is this true of how such motives operate in your life? Yes _____ No _____. Give an example to support your response.

Reference

Maslow, A. (1970). *Motivation and personality*. New York: HarperCollins.

Activity from Grasha, A. F. (1995). *Practical applications of psychology* (4th ed.). New York: HarperCollins. Reprinted by permission of Addison Wesley Longman Publishers, Inc.

Name _____

Date _____

ACTIVE LEARNING EXPERIENCE

8.2 MOODS

Ed Diener, Randy Larsen, Steven Levine, and Robert Emmons (1985) conducted a series of studies on affect. Although their research covered a longer period of time (up to ten weeks), their methods of collecting data may help you to understand your moods.

Using a scale from "0" (not at all) to "6" (extremely much), rate how you felt for each of the nine mood descriptions. Complete your rating at the end of each day. Do not read further until you complete your ratings for all seven days.

Day 1

[1]Unhappy

    0   1   2   3   4   5   6

(not at all)   (extremely much)

[2]Happy

    0   1   2   3   4   5   6

(not at all)   (extremely much)

[3]Depressed/blue

    0   1   2   3   4   5   6

(not at all)   (extremely much)

[4]Pleased

    0   1   2   3   4   5   6

(not at all)   (extremely much)

[5]Frustration

    0   1   2   3   4   5   6

(not at all)   (extremely much)

[6]Joyful

    0   1   2   3   4   5   6

(not at all)   (extremely much)

[7]Angry/hostile

    0   1   2   3   4   5   6

(not at all)   (extremely much)

[8]Enjoyment/fun

    0   1   2   3   4   5   6

(not at all)   (extremely much)

[9]Worried/anxious/fearful

    0   1   2   3   4   5   6

(not at all)   (extremely much)

Day 2

[1]Unhappy

	0	1	2	3	4	5	6	
(not at all)								(extremely much)

[2]Happy

	0	1	2	3	4	5	6	
(not at all)								(extremely much)

[3]Depressed/blue

	0	1	2	3	4	5	6	
(not at all)								(extremely much)

[4]Pleased

	0	1	2	3	4	5	6	
(not at all)								(extremely much)

[5]Frustration

	0	1	2	3	4	5	6	
(not at all)								(extremely much)

[6]Joyful

	0	1	2	3	4	5	6	
(not at all)								(extremely much)

[7]Angry/hostile

	0	1	2	3	4	5	6	
(not at all)								(extremely much)

[8]Enjoyment/fun

	0	1	2	3	4	5	6	
(not at all)								(extremely much)

[9]Worried/anxious/fearful

	0	1	2	3	4	5	6	
(not at all)								(extremely much)

Day 3

[1]Unhappy

	0	1	2	3	4	5	6	
(not at all)								(extremely much)

[2]Happy

	0	1	2	3	4	5	6	
(not at all)								(extremely much)

[3]Depressed/blue

	0	1	2	3	4	5	6	
(not at all)								(extremely much)

[4]Pleased

	0	1	2	3	4	5	6	
(not at all)								(extremely much)

[5]Frustration

	0	1	2	3	4	5	6	
(not at all)								(extremely much)

[6]Joyful	0 (not at all)	1	2	3	4	5	6 (extremely much)	

[7]Angry/hostile	0 (not at all)	1	2	3	4	5	6 (extremely much)	

[8]Enjoyment/fun	0 (not at all)	1	2	3	4	5	6 (extremely much)	

[9]Worried/anxious/fearful	0 (not at all)	1	2	3	4	5	6 (extremely much)	

Day 4

[1]Unhappy	0 (not at all)	1	2	3	4	5	6 (extremely much)	

[2]Happy	0 (not at all)	1	2	3	4	5	6 (extremely much)	

[3]Depressed/blue	0 (not at all)	1	2	3	4	5	6 (extremely much)	

[4]Pleased	0 (not at all)	1	2	3	4	5	6 (extremely much)	

[5]Frustration	0 (not at all)	1	2	3	4	5	6 (extremely much)	

[6]Joyful	0 (not at all)	1	2	3	4	5	6 (extremely much)	

[7]Angry/hostile	0 (not at all)	1	2	3	4	5	6 (extremely much)	

[8]Enjoyment/fun	0 (not at all)	1	2	3	4	5	6 (extremely much)	

[9]Worried/anxious/fearful	0 (not at all)	1	2	3	4	5	6 (extremely much)	

Day 5

| [1]Unhappy | 0 | 1 | 2 | 3 | 4 | 5 | 6 |
| | (not at all) | | | | | (extremely much) | |

| [2]Happy | 0 | 1 | 2 | 3 | 4 | 5 | 6 |
| | (not at all) | | | | | (extremely much) | |

| [3]Depressed/blue | 0 | 1 | 2 | 3 | 4 | 5 | 6 |
| | (not at all) | | | | | (extremely much) | |

| [4]Pleased | 0 | 1 | 2 | 3 | 4 | 5 | 6 |
| | (not at all) | | | | | (extremely much) | |

| [5]Frustration | 0 | 1 | 2 | 3 | 4 | 5 | 6 |
| | (not at all) | | | | | (extremely much) | |

| [6]Joyful | 0 | 1 | 2 | 3 | 4 | 5 | 6 |
| | (not at all) | | | | | (extremely much) | |

| [7]Angry/hostile | 0 | 1 | 2 | 3 | 4 | 5 | 6 |
| | (not at all) | | | | | (extremely much) | |

| [8]Enjoyment/fun | 0 | 1 | 2 | 3 | 4 | 5 | 6 |
| | (not at all) | | | | | (extremely much) | |

| [9]Worried/anxious/fearful | 0 | 1 | 2 | 3 | 4 | 5 | 6 |
| | (not at all) | | | | | (extremely much) | |

Day 6

| [1]Unhappy | 0 | 1 | 2 | 3 | 4 | 5 | 6 |
| | (not at all) | | | | | (extremely much) | |

| [2]Happy | 0 | 1 | 2 | 3 | 4 | 5 | 6 |
| | (not at all) | | | | | (extremely much) | |

| [3]Depressed/blue | 0 | 1 | 2 | 3 | 4 | 5 | 6 |
| | (not at all) | | | | | (extremely much) | |

| [4]Pleased | 0 | 1 | 2 | 3 | 4 | 5 | 6 |
| | (not at all) | | | | | (extremely much) | |

| [5]Frustration | 0 | 1 | 2 | 3 | 4 | 5 | 6 |
| | (not at all) | | | | | (extremely much) | |

[6]Joyful

0   1   2   3   4   5   6

(not at all)   (extremely much)

[7]Angry/hostile

0   1   2   3   4   5   6

(not at all)   (extremely much)

[8]Enjoyment/fun

0   1   2   3   4   5   6

(not at all)   (extremely much)

[9]Worried/anxious/fearful

0   1   2   3   4   5   6

(not at all)   (extremely much)

Day 7

[1]Unhappy

0   1   2   3   4   5   6

(not at all)   (extremely much)

[2]Happy

0   1   2   3   4   5   6

(not at all)   (extremely much)

[3]Depressed/blue

0   1   2   3   4   5   6

(not at all)   (extremely much)

[4]Pleased

0   1   2   3   4   5   6

(not at all)   (extremely much)

[5]Frustration

0   1   2   3   4   5   6

(not at all)   (extremely much)

[6]Joyful

0   1   2   3   4   5   6

(not at all)   (extremely much)

[7]Angry/hostile

0   1   2   3   4   5   6

(not at all)   (extremely much)

[8]Enjoyment/fun

0   1   2   3   4   5   6

(not at all)   (extremely much)

[9]Worried/anxious/fearful

0   1   2   3   4   5   6

(not at all)   (extremely much)

When you finish your ratings for the *week*, total the positive affect items (#2, 4, 6, & 8) and the negative affect items (#1, 3, 5, 7, & 9) separately.

Day	Positive Total	Negative Total
1	/4 =	/5 =
2	/4 =	/5 =
3	/4 =	/5 =
4	/4 =	/5 =
5	/4 =	/5 =
6	/4 =	/5 =
7	/4 =	/5 =

Is this a good indicator of how you "generally" feel? If so, why? If not, why?

What do you attribute these feelings to?

Are you satisfied with your general mood? If so, why? If not, why (and what can you do to change this situation)?

Reference

Diener, E., Larsen, R. J., Levine, S., & Emmons, R. A. (1985). Intensity and frequency: Dimensions underlying positive and negative affect. *Journal of Personality and Social Psychology, 49*, 1253–1265.

Name _____

Date _____

ACTIVE LEARNING EXPERIENCE

8.3 LIFESTYLE AND HEALTH

Paul Insel, Walton Roth, L. McKay Rollins, and Ray Petersen (1998) adapted the following questionnaire from one created by the U.S. Public Health Service. [From *Core concepts in health, brief edition*, 8th edition. Copyright © 1998 by Mayfield Publishing Company. Reprinted by permission of the publisher.] The behaviors covered in the test are recommended for most Americans. (Some of them may not apply to people with certain diseases or disabilities, or to pregnant women who may require special advice from their physicians.) After you take the quiz, add up your score for each section.

	Almost Always	Sometimes	Never

Tobacco Use

If you never use tobacco, enter a score of 10 for this section and go to the next section.

		Almost Always	Sometimes	Never
1.	I avoid using tobacco.	2	1	0
2.	I smoke only low tar and nicotine cigarettes *or* I smoke a pipe or cigar *or* I use smokeless tobacco.	2	1	0

Tobacco Score: _____

Alcohol and Other Drugs

		Almost Always	Sometimes	Never
1.	I avoid alcohol *or* I drink no more than 1 (women) or 2 (men) drinks a day.	4	1	0
2.	I avoid using alcohol or other drugs as a way of handling stressful situations or problems in my life.	2	1	0
3.	I am careful not to drink alcohol when taking medications, such as for colds or allergies, or when pregnant.	2	1	0
4.	I read and follow the label directions when using prescribed and over-the-counter drugs.	2	1	0

Alcohol and Other Drugs Score: _____

	Almost Always	Sometimes	Never

Nutrition

1. I eat a variety of foods each day, including five or more servings of fruits and vegetables.

	3	1	0
2. I limit the amount of fat and saturated fat in my diet.	3	1	0
3. I avoid skipping meals.	2	1	0
4. I limit the amount of salt and sugar I eat.	2	1	0

Nutrition Score: _____

Exercise/Fitness

1. I engage in moderate exercise for 20 to 60 minutes, three to five times a week.

	4	1	0
2. I maintain a healthy weight, avoiding overweight and underweight.	2	1	0

3. I do exercises to develop muscular strength and endurance at least twice a week.

	2	1	0

4. I spend some of my leisure time participating in physical activities such as gardening, bowling, golf, or baseball.

	2	1	0

Exercise/Fitness Score: _____

Emotional Health

1. I enjoy being a student and I have a job or do other work that I like.

	2	1	0
2. I find it easy to relax and express my feelings freely.	2	1	0
3. I manage stress well.	2	1	0

4. I have close friends, relatives, or others I can talk to about personal matters and call on for help.

	2	1	0

5. I participate in group activities (such as church and community organizations) or hobbies that I enjoy.

	2	1	0

Emotional Health Score: _____

	Almost Always	Sometimes	Never

Safety

		Almost Always	Sometimes	Never
1.	I wear a safety belt while riding in a car.	2	1	0
2.	I avoid driving while under the influence of alcohol or other drugs.	2	1	0
3.	I obey traffic rules and the speed limit when driving.	2	1	0
4.	I read and follow instructions on the labels of potentially harmful products or substances, such as household cleaners, poisons, and electrical appliances.	2	1	0
5.	I avoid smoking in bed.	2	1	0

Safety Score: _____

Disease Prevention

		Almost Always	Sometimes	Never
1.	I know the warning signs of cancer, diabetes, heart attack, and stroke.	2	1	0
2.	I avoid overexposure to the sun and use sunscreens.	2	1	0
3.	I get recommended medical screening tests (such as blood pressure checks and Pap tests), immunization, and booster shots.	2	1	0
4.	I practice monthly breast/testicle self-exams.	2	1	0
5.	I am not sexually active *or* I have sex with only one mutually faithful, uninfected partner *or* I always engage in safer sex (using condoms) *and* I do not share needles to inject drugs.	2	1	0

Disease Prevention Score: _____

What Your Scores Mean

Scores of 9 and 10   Excellent! Your answers show that you are aware of the importance of this area to wellness. More important, you are putting your knowledge to work for you by practicing good health habits. As long as you continue to do so, this area should not pose a serious health risk. It's likely that you are setting an example for your family and friends to follow. Since you earned a very high test score on this part of the test, you may want to focus on other areas where your scores indicate room for improvement.

Scores of 6–8   Your health practices in this area are good, but there is room for improvement. Look again at the items you answered with a "Sometimes" or "Never." Even a small change can often help you achieve better health.

Scores of 3–5   Your health risks are showing! You may need more information about the risks you are facing and about why it is important for you to change these behaviors. Perhaps you need help in deciding how to successfully make the changes you desire.

Scores of 0–2   Your answers show that you may be taking serious and unnecessary risks with your health. Perhaps you are not aware of the risks and what to do about them. You can easily get the information and help you need to improve, if you wish. The next step is up to you.

Is your score an accurate reflection of how you see yourself?

How do you feel about your score?

What changes can you make to improve your health?

Reference

Insel, P. M., Roth, W. T., Rollins, L. M., & Petersen, R. A. (1998). *Core concepts in health* (Brief 8th Ed.). Mountain View, CA: Mayfield.

CHAPTER 9

DEVELOPMENT

Name _____

Date _____

ACTIVE LEARNING EXPERIENCE

9.1 INTIMACY

Erik Erikson's (1963) psychosocial theory of development progresses through eight stages, each important for the development of a dimension of personality (e.g., trust versus mistrust, industry versus inferiority, intimacy versus isolation). According to Erikson, each stage reflects a conflict involving emerging personal needs and social demands. While crisis is inevitable, its positive or negative resolution impacts future development.

The following questionnaire was designed by Rhona Ochse and Cornelis Plug (1986) to assess Erikson's sixth stage of development—Intimacy versus Isolation. It should give you an idea of where you stand in comparison to your peers with respect to resolving this crisis.

The following questions are presented in the form of statements. Indicate the extent that each of these statements applies to you by circling one of the following responses: Never (N), Occasionally (O), Fairly Often (FO), or Very Often (VO).

		N	O	FO	VO
1.	I feel that no-one has ever known the real me.	__	__	__	__
2.	I have a feeling of complete "togetherness" with someone.	__	__	__	__
3.	I feel it is better to remain free than to become committed to marriage for life.	__	__	__	__
4.	I share my private thoughts with someone.	__	__	__	__
5.	I feel as though I am alone in the world.	__	__	__	__
6.	Someone shares my joys and sorrows.	__	__	__	__
7.	I feel nobody really cares about me.	__	__	__	__
8.	I feel embarrassed when people tell me about their personal problems.	__	__	__	__

Each response receives a score of 1 through 4. Item numbers 2, 4, and 6 are scored as follows: never = 1, occasionally = 2, fairly often = 3, and very often = 4. Item numbers 1, 3, 5, 7, and 8 are scored in the reverse direction (e.g., never = 4, very often = 1).

Total your score across all 8 items. _____

I have found a mean of 24 and a standard deviation of 4 for college students. Since most students fall between 20 and 28, you can compare your progress toward achieving a sense of intimacy.

In examining the individual items, which ones are most problematic for you? Why?

How would you go about trying to accomplish change?

References

Erikson, E. (1963). *Childhood and society.* New York: Norton.

Ochse, R., & Plug, C. (1986). Cross-cultural investigation of the validity of Erikson's theory of personality development. *Journal of Personality and Social Psychology, 50,* 1240–1252.

Scale from Ochse, R., & Plug, C. (1986). Cross-cultural investigation of the validity of Erikson's theory of personality development. *Journal of Personality and Social Psychology, 50,* 1240–1252 (Copyright © 1986 by the American Psychological Association. Reprinted with permission.).

Name _____

Date _____

ACTIVE LEARNING EXPERIENCE

9.2 TEMPERAMENT

Arnold Buss and Robert Plomin (1984) have conducted extensive research on temperament—inherited personality traits present in early childhood. In an extension of research on infants and children, they developed the EAS Temperament Survey for Adults.

Before reading further, complete the questionnaire below. [From Buss, A. H, & Plomin, R. (1984). *Temperament: Early developing personality traits*. Hillsdale, NJ: Copyright © 1984, Lawrence Erlbaum Associates, Publishers. Reprinted with permission.]

Rate each of the items on a scale of 1 (not characteristic or typical of yourself) to 5 (very characteristic or typical of yourself).

1.	I like to be with people.	1	2	3	4	5
2.	I usually seem to be in a hurry.	1	2	3	4	5
3.	I am easily frightened.	1	2	3	4	5
4.	I frequently get distressed.	1	2	3	4	5
5.	When displeased, I let people know it right away.	1	2	3	4	5
6.	I am something of a loner.	1	2	3	4	5
7.	I like to keep busy all the time.	1	2	3	4	5
8.	I am known as hot-blooded and quick-tempered.	1	2	3	4	5
9.	I often feel frustrated.	1	2	3	4	5
10.	My life is fast paced.	1	2	3	4	5
11.	Everyday events make me troubled and fretful.	1	2	3	4	5
12.	I often feel insecure.	1	2	3	4	5
13.	There are many things that annoy me.	1	2	3	4	5
14.	When I get scared, I panic.	1	2	3	4	5
15.	I prefer working with others rather than alone.	1	2	3	4	5
16.	I get emotionally upset easily.	1	2	3	4	5
17.	I often feel as if I'm bursting with energy.	1	2	3	4	5
18.	It takes a lot to make me mad.	1	2	3	4	5
19.	I have fewer fears than most people my age.	1	2	3	4	5
20.	I find people more stimulating than anything else.	1	2	3	4	5

Scoring instructions: Reverse items 6, 18, and 19 by setting 5=1, 4=2, 3=3, 2=4, and 1=5. Then add the scores for the four items on each of the 5 scales and divide each scale score by 4 (number of items per scale) in order to interpret scores in terms of the 1–5 scale.

Scales

Emotionality
    Distress: Items 4, 9, 11, and 16   =   _____
    Fearfulness: Items 3, 12, 14, and 19   =   _____
    Anger: Items 5, 8, 13 and 18   =   _____

Activity
    Items 2, 7, 10, and 17   =   _____

Sociability
    Items 1, 6, 15, and 20   =   _____

Buss and Plomin reported the following means and standard deviations for *women*: Distress (Mean = 2.52, SD = 0.86), Fearfulness (Mean = 2.65, SD = 0.73), Anger (Mean = 2.57, SD = 0.82), Activity (Mean = 3.35, SD = 0.69), and Sociability (Mean = 3.81, SD = 0.73).

They reported the following for *men:* Distress (Mean = 2.43, SD = 0.65), Fearfulness (Mean = 2.23, SD = 0.71), Anger (Mean = 2.70, SD = 0.77), Activity (Mean = 3.20, SD = 0.62), and Sociability (Mean = 3.65, SD = 0.81).

How well did this scale reflect these aspects of your personality? Explain

    Emotionality:

Activity:

Sociability:

Would you say that with respect to each of these dimensions "you have always been this way"? Or have you noticed pronounced changes in emotionality, activity, and/or sociability since your childhood years? Explain.

Reference

Buss, A. H., & Plomin R. (1984). *Temperament: Early developing personality traits*. Hillsdale, NJ: Erlbaum.

Name _____

Date _____

ACTIVE LEARNING EXPERIENCE

9.3   REASONING

Deanne Kuhn and Joann Brannock (1977) devised a Piagetian problem-solving situation that closely parallels everyday experience and decision making. The following adaptation of their experiment should shed light on how you go about drawing conclusions based on your observations in various situations.

Examine the four plants below with their weekly rations:

Plant 1

Eight oz. of water
Plant food A

Plant 2

Eight oz. of water
Plant food B
One oz. of leaf lotion

Plant 3

Four oz. of water
Plant food A
One oz. of leaf lotion

Plant 4

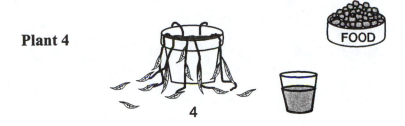

4

Four oz. of water
Plant food B

I just purchased another one of those plants and will begin growing it with the following weekly rations:

Four oz. of water
Plant food A

How do you think this plant will turn out?

Why? (Be specific and detailed in your answer to reflect your reasoning process.)

Do you think the leaf lotion has anything to do with how this plant will turn out?

Why? (Be specific and detailed in your answer to reflect your reasoning process.)

Kuhn and Brannock (1977) described this task as one in which the individual must utilize the isolation-of-variables scheme common in scientific reasoning and considered a hallmark of formal operational thought. Cindy Lightfoot, who uses this task in her courses, (personal communication, 1998) noted that this problem examines one's ability to isolate a relevant (operative) variable when it occurs with a number of other, nonoperative variables. To approach this problem from the formal operational level, one must (a) logically or systematically *isolate* the relevant variable and (b) systematically *exclude* the other variables.

Judge your performance by comparing your approach to the following guidelines:

Category 1:   not isolating variables

Category 2:   isolating a relevant variable but not excluding the irrelevant ones

Category 3:   both isolating the correct variable and excluding the others

For example, if you thought that two variables were important (e.g., water and plant food) but did not compare them across conditions, your response would be in Category 1. If you thought two variables were important and described their presence or absence across at least two conditions, *or* if you thought one variable was important, but another might be too, your response would be in Category 2. If you isolated the *one* relevant variable (plant food) *and* described why the others (especially the leaf lotion) were not important, your response would be in Category 3. (From C. Lightfoot, personal communication, 1998.)

Kuhn and Brannock (1977) noted that responses in Category 2 were regarded as transitional between concrete and formal operations. Category 3 responses reflect formal operational thought.

How would you evaluate your reasoning abilities on this task?

Describe a similar situation you might encounter in your daily life and how you would go about making a decision.

Reference

Kuhn, D., & Brannock, J. (1977). Development of the isolation of variables scheme in experimental and "natural experiment" contexts. *Developmental Psychology, 13*, 9–14.

CHAPTER 10

PERSONALITY

Name _____

Date _____

ACTIVE LEARNING EXPERIENCE

10.1 SELF-RATINGS

Martin Bolt (1996) designed an interesting self-assessment activity that allows you to reflect on many of your personal characteristics. [From Instructor's manual to accompany Myers *Social Psychology* (5th ed.) (1996). New York: McGraw-Hill. Reprinted with permission of the McGraw-Hill Companies.] Before reading further, follow the directions below.

Instructions: Compared with other college students of the same class level and sex as yourself, how would you rate yourself on the following characteristics? Use the following scale in marking your responses.

1 = considerably well below average
2 = well below average
3 = below average
4 = slightly below average
5 = average
6 = slightly above average
7 = above average
8 = well above average
9 = considerably well above average

_____ 1. leadership ability

_____ 2. athletic ability

_____ 3. ability to get along with others

_____ 4. tolerance

_____ 5. energy level

_____ 6. helpfulness

_____ 7. responsibility

_____ 8. creativeness

_____ 9. patience

_____ 10. trustworthiness

_____ 11. sincerity

_____ 12. thoughtfulness

_____ 13. cooperativeness

_____ 14. reasonableness

_____ 15. intelligence

After completing the Self-Rating questionnaire, calculate your mean score by adding up all 15 items and dividing by 15.

Score = _____

Previous demonstrations indicate that most students will have mean ratings above the average of 5.0. This self-serving bias, termed the better-than-average phenomenon, suggests that almost all of us see ourselves as better than average.

Anthony Greenwald (1995) linked this behavior to a bias called "beneffectance," which is part of an elaborate system designed to protect the "self." "In judging the self compared to others, we see ourselves as having more than our fair share of good qualities and also more than others are inclined to credit us with" (p. 6). He went on to state that this "system" impacts many aspects of our lives. Most notably, "in observing others, we most easily notice characteristics that are central to our own personalities. . . . we readily believe that successes fairly reflect our abilities. . . . we avoid taking responsibility for failure, chalking it up instead to uncontrollable circumstances, and we smoothly reconstruct memories of our past to make it . . . consistent with our present self-image" (p. 6). Sound Freudian (or at least Neo-Freudian)?

Does the knowledge of this and other biases affect your view of your "self" in various situations? Explain.

References

Bolt, M. (1996). *Instructor's manual to accompany Myers Social Psychology* (5th ed.). New York: McGraw-Hill.

Greenwald, A. G. (1995). Getting (my) self into social psychology. In G. G. Brannigan & M. R. Merrens (Eds.). *The Social psychologists: Research adventures* (pp. 2–16) New York: McGraw-Hill.

Name _____

Date _____

ACTIVE LEARNING EXPERIENCE

10.2 FIVE-FACTOR MODEL

Robert McCrae and Paul Costa (1987) advanced a theory that utilizes five factors to explain personality. The following questionnaire briefly examines some aspects of each of the five factors. You can take the self-rating form and (if you are brave enough) the peer-rating form. For the peer rating, ask someone who knows you well (other than a relative or romantic partner) to rate you on the dimensions indicated. You can then compare how you see yourself with how another person sees you. You might be surprised!

Self-Rating

Rate yourself on the following dimensions by circling the appropriate number on the five-point scale.

1. Down to Earth   Imaginative
       1   2   3   4   5

2. Lazy   Hard Working
       1   2   3   4   5

3. Secure   Insecure
       1   2   3   4   5

4. Reserved   Affectionate
       1   2   3   4   5

5. Callous   Sympathetic
       1   2   3   4   5

6. Comfortable   Self-conscious
       1   2   3   4   5

7. Uncooperative   Helpful
       1   2   3   4   5

8. Narrow Interests

    1   2   3   4   Broad Interests

    1   2   3   4   5

9. Quiet — Talkative

    1   2   3   4   5

10. Negligent — Conscientious

    1   2   3   4   5

11. Calm — Worrying

    1   2   3   4   5

12. Aloof — Friendly

    1   2   3   4   5

13. Conventional — Original

    1   2   3   4   5

14. Aimless — Ambitious

    1   2   3   4   5

15. Vengeful — Forgiving

    1   2   3   4   5

16. Even-tempered — Temperamental

    1   2   3   4   5

17. Retiring — Sociable

    1   2   3   4   5

18. Quitting — Persevering

    1   2   3   4   5

19. Unadventurous — Daring

    1   2   3   4   5

20. Irritable — Good-natured

    1   2   3   4   5

Peer-Rating

Rate _____ on the following dimension by circling the appropriate number on the five-point scale.

1. Down to Earth   Imaginative
      1   2   3   4   5

2. Lazy   Hard Working
      1   2   3   4   5

3. Secure   Insecure
      1   2   3   4   5

4. Reserved   Affectionate
      1   2   3   4   5

5. Callous   Sympathetic
      1   2   3   4   5

6. Comfortable   Self-conscious
      1   2   3   4   5

7. Uncooperative   Helpful
      1   2   3   4   5

8. Narrow Interests   Broad Interests
      1   2   3   4   5

9. Quiet   Talkative
      1   2   3   4   5

10. Negligent   Conscientious
       1   2   3   4   5

11. Calm   Worrying
       1   2   3   4   5

12. Aloof   Friendly
       1   2   3   4   5

13. Conventional

| 1 | 2 | 3 | 4 | Original 5 |

14. Aimless

| 1 | 2 | 3 | 4 | Ambitious 5 |

15. Vengeful

| 1 | 2 | 3 | 4 | Forgiving 5 |

16. Even-tempered

| 1 | 2 | 3 | 4 | Temperamental 5 |

17. Retiring

| 1 | 2 | 3 | 4 | Sociable 5 |

18. Quitting

| 1 | 2 | 3 | 4 | Persevering 5 |

19. Unadventurous

| 1 | 2 | 3 | 4 | Daring 5 |

20. Irritable

| 1 | 2 | 3 | 4 | Good-natured 5 |

Scoring: Total your scores for each of the five dimensions and divide each by 4.

Openness to Experience (0) :   1, 8, 13, and 19

Conscientiousness (C) :   2, 10, 14, and 18

Extraversion (E) :   4, 9, 12, and 17

Agreeableness (A):   5, 7, 15, and 20

Neuroticism (N) :   3, 6, 11, and 16

	Self-Ratings	Peer-Ratings
O	_____	_____
C	_____	_____
E	_____	_____
A	_____	_____
N	_____	_____

These five dimensions are thought by many to be "basic" descriptions of personality. In interpreting your scores, you can get an idea of where you fall on each dimension by how far in either direction your score is from the midpoint (3) of the scale. The higher the score, the higher you are on that dimension.

In what ways might these personality traits affect your functioning in the following areas:

Your personal life:

Your social life:

Academics:

Vocational choice:

How did the self- and peer ratings compare? Were you surprised by any of the ratings?

If there were differences in the ratings, how would you account for them?

Reference

McCrae, R. R., & Costa, P. T., Jr. (1987). Validation of the five-factor model of personality across instruments and observers. *Journal of Personality and Social Psychology, 52,* 81–90.

Scale drawn from material in McCrae, R. R., & Costa, P. T., Jr. (1987). Validation of the five-factor model of personality across instruments and observers. *Journal of Personality and Social Psychology, 52,* 81–90.

Name _____

Date _____

ACTIVE LEARNING EXPERIENCE

10.3   SELF-ACTUALIZATION

Self-actualization refers to the life-long process of realizing our potentialities and becoming fully functioning persons. It is a central theme in humanistic psychology.

The following questionnaire is one attempt to measure this elusive concept. To determine how you stand in your progress toward this goal, follow the instructions below.

Please indicate to what extent you agree or disagree with each of the following statements by placing an X on the appropriate line.

	Strongly Agree	Agree	Somewhat Agree	Somewhat Disagree	Disagree	Strongly Disagree
1. I do not feel ashamed of any of my emotions.	____	____	____	____	____	____
2. I feel I must do what others expect of me.	____	____	____	____	____	____
3. I believe that people are essentially good and can be trusted.	____	____	____	____	____	____
4. I feel free to be angry at those I love.	____	____	____	____	____	____
5. It is always necessary that others approve of what I do.	____	____	____	____	____	____
6. I don't accept my own weaknesses.	____	____	____	____	____	____
7. I can like people without having to approve of them.	____	____	____	____	____	____
8. I fear failure.	____	____	____	____	____	____
9. I avoid attempts to analyze and simplify complex domains.	____	____	____	____	____	____
10. It is better to be yourself than to be popular.	____	____	____	____	____	____
11. I have no mission in life to which I feel especially dedicated.	____	____	____	____	____	____
12. I can express my feelings even when they may result in undesirable consequences.	____	____	____	____	____	____
13. I do not feel responsible to help anybody.	____	____	____	____	____	____
14. I am bothered by fears of being inadequate.	____	____	____	____	____	____
15. I am loved because I give love.	____	____	____	____	____	____

INTERPRETATION

Each response receives a score of 1 through 6. Items 1, 3, 4, 7, 10, 12, and 15 are scored as follows: strongly disagree = 1, disagree = 2, somewhat disagree = 3, somewhat agree = 4, agree = 5, and strongly agree = 6. Items 2, 5, 6, 8, 9, 11, 13, and 14 are scored in the reverse direction (e.g., strongly disagree = 6, strongly agree = 1).

Total your scores across the 15 items. The higher the score, the more self-actualized you are at this time.

Score =

The following table will show you how your score compares to those of other college students.

SCORE	PERCENTILE
77	99
76	95
75	90
73	80
71	70
69	60
67	50
65	40
60	30
55	20
53	10
52	5
51	1

Looking back at your responses to specific questions, identify areas where you are not yet realizing your potential.

Why do you think this is the case?

What can you do to become more fully functioning in these areas?

Reference

Scale from Jones, A., & Crandall, R. (1986). Validation of a short index of self-actualization. *Personality and Social Psychology Bulletin, 12(1),* 63–73. Copyright © 1986. Reprinted with permission of Sage Publications, Inc.

CHAPTER 11

PSYCHOLOGICAL DISORDERS

Name _____

Date _____

ACTIVE LEARNING EXPERIENCE

11.1 OBSESSIVE-COMPULSIVE PERSONALITY

Gerald Gibb, James Bailey, Randall Best, and Thomas Lambirth (1983) designed a questionnaire to assess obsessive-compulsive traits. To assess this aspect of your personality, complete the following questionnaire by answering either True or False to each question.

_____ 1. I feel compelled to do things I don't want to do.
_____ 2. I usually check things that I know I have already done.
_____ 3. I can walk 30 miles in an hour.
_____ 4. I often do things I don't want to do because I cannot resist doing them.
_____ 5. I seldom keep a daily routine.
_____ 6. I feel compelled to always complete what I am doing.
_____ 7. I often feel the need to double check what I do.
_____ 8. I'd rather do things the same way all the time.
_____ 9. I seldom have recurring thoughts.
_____ 10. I seldom am compelled to do something I don't want to do.
_____ 11. I don't feel uncomfortable and uneasy when I don't do things my usual way.
_____ 12. If I don't feel like doing something it won't bother me not to do it.
_____ 13. I usually never feel the need to be organized.
_____ 14. I am uneasy about keeping a rigid time schedule.
_____ 15. My birthday comes once a year.
_____ 16. I am often compelled to do some things I do not want to do.
_____ 17. I like to keep a rigid daily routine.
_____ 18. I believe there is a place for everything and everything in its place.
_____ 19. I seldom check things I know I have already done.
_____ 20. I am not obsessed with details.
_____ 21. I often have recurring thoughts.
_____ 22. I like to do things differently each time.

Scoring: For items 1, 2, 4, 6, 7, 8, 16 17, 18, and 21 give yourself one point for each one answered true.

For items 5, 9, 10, 11, 12, 13, 14, 19, 20, and 22 give yourself one point for each one answered false.

Items 3 and 15 are validity check items, and are not counted.

Total your points

Score: _____

The authors reported a mean of 11.22 and a standard deviation of 3.96 for college undergraduates.

How well did this scale assess the degree of obsessiveness/compulsivity of your personality? Explain.

In what ways might obsessive-compulsive traits benefit you in your daily life?

In what ways might obsessive-compulsive traits hinder you in your daily life?

Reference

Gibb, G. D., Bailey, J. R., Best, R. H., & Lambirth, T. T. (1983). The measurement of the obsessive compulsive personality. *Educational and Psychological Measurement, 43*, 1233–1238.

Name _____

Date _____

ACTIVE LEARNING EXPERIENCE

11.2 FEARS

James Geer (1965) developed the following survey to measure fear—"a negative emotional response evoked by a relatively specific stimulus" (p. 45). Before reading further, complete this survey.

Instructions: For each item circle the intensity of the fear you feel toward the object or situation noted in this item.

1 None	2 Very Little	3 A Little	4 Some	5 Much	6 Very Much		7 Terror

		1	2	3	4	5	6	7
1.	Sharp object	1	2	3	4	5	6	7
2.	Being a passenger in a car	1	2	3	4	5	6	7
3.	Dead bodies	1	2	3	4	5	6	7
4.	Suffocating	1	2	3	4	5	6	7
5.	Failing a test	1	2	3	4	5	6	7
6.	Looking foolish	1	2	3	4	5	6	7
7.	Being a passenger in an airplane	1	2	3	4	5	6	7
8.	Worms	1	2	3	4	5	6	7
9.	Arguing with parents	1	2	3	4	5	6	7
10.	Rats and mice	1	2	3	4	5	6	7
11.	Life after death	1	2	3	4	5	6	7
12.	Hypodermic needles	1	2	3	4	5	6	7
13.	Being criticized	1	2	3	4	5	6	7
14.	Meeting someone for the first time	1	2	3	4	5	6	7
15.	Roller coasters	1	2	3	4	5	6	7
16.	Being alone	1	2	3	4	5	6	7
17.	Making mistakes	1	2	3	4	5	6	7
18.	Being misunderstood	1	2	3	4	5	6	7
19.	Death	1	2	3	4	5	6	7
20.	Being in a fight	1	2	3	4	5	6	7
21.	Crowded places	1	2	3	4	5	6	7
22.	Blood	1	2	3	4	5	6	7
23.	Heights	1	2	3	4	5	6	7
24.	Being a leader	1	2	3	4	5	6	7
25.	Swimming alone	1	2	3	4	5	6	7
26.	Illness	1	2	3	4	5	6	7
27.	Being with drunks	1	2	3	4	5	6	7
28.	Illness or injury to loved ones	1	2	3	4	5	6	7
29.	Being self-conscious	1	2	3	4	5	6	7
30.	Driving a car	1	2	3	4	5	6	7
31.	Meeting authority	1	2	3	4	5	6	7

1	2	3	4	5	6	7
None	Very Little	A Little	Some	Much	Very Much	Terror

32. Mental illness	1	2	3	4	5	6	7
33. Closed places	1	2	3	4	5	6	7
34. Boating	1	2	3	4	5	6	7
35. Spiders	1	2	3	4	5	6	7
36. Thunderstorms	1	2	3	4	5	6	7
37. Not being a success	1	2	3	4	5	6	7
38. God	1	2	3	4	5	6	7
39. Snakes	1	2	3	4	5	6	7
40. Cemeteries	1	2	3	4	5	6	7
41. Speaking before a group	1	2	3	4	5	6	7
42. Seeing a fight	1	2	3	4	5	6	7
43. Death of a loved one	1	2	3	4	5	6	7
44. Dark places	1	2	3	4	5	6	7
45. Strange dogs	1	2	3	4	5	6	7
46. Deep water	1	2	3	4	5	6	7
47. Being with a member of the opposite sex	1	2	3	4	5	6	7
48 Stinging insects	1	2	3	4	5	6	7
49. Untimely or early death	1	2	3	4	5	6	7
50. Losing a job	1	2	3	4	5	6	7
51. Auto accidents	1	2	3	4	5	6	7

Scoring: Add up the scores for the 51 items.

Score _____

Geer (1965) reported a mean total score of 75.78 (standard deviation = 33.84) for undergraduate men, and a mean total score of 100.16 (standard deviation = 36.11) for undergraduate women.

Note your most feared stimuli:

1.   6.
2.   7.
3.   8.
4.   9.
5.   10.

Geer (1965) reported that the following were most feared by men:

1. Death of a loved one.
2. Failing a test.
3. Illness or injury to loved ones.
4. Looking foolish/not being a success.
5. Speaking before a group.
6. Making mistakes.
7. Auto accidents.
8. Being criticized.
9. Snakes.
10. Death.

The following were most feared by women:

1. Death of a loved one.
2. Illness or injury to loved ones.
3. Failing a test.
4. Snakes
5. Auto accidents.
6. Looking foolish.
7. Speaking before a group.
8. Untimely or early death.
9. Being with drunks.
10. Making mistakes

What impact does fear have on your day-to-day activities?

Do your fears limit you from experiencing life in any way?

Reference

Geer, J. H. (1965). The development of a scale to measure fear. *Behaviour Research and Therapy, 3,* 45–53.

Scale from Geer, J. H. (1965). The development of a scale to measure fear. *Behaviour Research and Therapy, 3,* 45–53. Reprinted with permission of Elsevier Science.

Name _____

Date _____

ACTIVE LEARNING EXPERIENCE

11.3 DEPRESSION SCALE

Depression is a serious problem in this country, especially among college students. To assess yourself for depression, complete the following scale developed by William Zung (1965).

Instructions: Rate each of the items as to how it applies to you now.

The Self-Rating Depression Scale

	A Little of the Time	Some of the Time	Good Part of the Time	Most of the Time
1. I feel down-hearted and blue.				
2. Morning is when I feel the best.				
3. I have crying spells or feel like it.				
4. I have trouble sleeping at night.				
5. I eat as much as I used to.				
6. I still enjoy sex.				
7. I notice that I am losing weight.				
8. I have trouble with constipation.				
9. My heart beats faster than usual.				
10. I get tired for no reason.				
11. My mind is as clear as it used to be.				
12. I find it easy to do the things I used to.				
13. I am restless and can't keep still.				
14. I feel hopeful about the future.				
15. I am more irritable than usual.				
16. I find it easy to make decisions.				
17. I feel that I am useful and needed.				
18. My life is pretty full.				
19. I feel that others would be better off if I were dead.				
20. I still enjoy the things I used to do.				

Scoring: Item numbers 1, 3, 4, 7, 8, 9, 10, 13, 15, and 19 are scored as follows: a little of the time = 1, some of the time = 2, good part of the time = 3, and most of the time = 4. For item numbers 2, 5, 6, 11, 12, 14, 16, 17, 18, and 20 scores for those categories are reversed (e.g., a little of the time = 4, some of the time = 3, good part of the time = 2, and most of the time = 1).

To figure your score, add your scores for all 20 items:

Score = _____

Scores can range from 20 to 80. The higher the score the greater the depression. Zung (1965) reported a mean of 26 with a range from 20 to 34 for his control group, and a mean of 59 with a range from 50 to 72 for depressed patients. [Note that dieting can raise your score, because two items (#5 and #7) deal with eating. Take this into consideration when you are interpreting your score.]

How does your score compare with your impressions of your current affect and your physiological and psychological functioning? [If you are concerned about your score, you should discuss it with a mental health professional.]

Reference

Zung, W.W.K. (1965). A self-rating depression scale. *Archives of General Psychiatry, 12*, 63–70. Scale reprinted with permission of the American Medical Association.

CHAPTER 12

THERAPIES

Name _____

Date _____

ACTIVE LEARNING EXPERIENCE

12.1 BEHAVIOR MODIFICATION

Probably the best way to understand the behavioral perspective on therapy is to implement a program to modify your own behavior. Follow the following guidelines.

1. Choose a target behavior you wish to change. Here are some behaviors that students frequently select (from Merrens and Brannigan, 1998, p. 157).

smoking	fears
eating	smiling
studying	exercise
arguing	using profanities
nail biting	socializing
hair twirling	telephoning
looking in mirror	sleeping

What is your target behavior: _____

2. Clearly specify which aspect of your behavior you wish to monitor: frequency (how often it occurs) or duration (how long it occurs).

Choose your measure: _____

3. Establish a baseline record of your typical behavior before starting your program. Keep track of the frequency or duration of the behavior for one week.

Data

day 1 _____
day 2 _____
day 3 _____
day 4 _____
day 5 _____
day 6 _____
day 7 _____

What is your baseline (average): _____

4. Set goals for yourself. Look for gradual improvement over time. One of the biggest problems people have is that they set goals too high, don't reach them, get frustrated, and give up. It is better to start slowly, and gradually increase goals over a period of at least a few weeks.

Goals: Week 1 _____
: Week 2 _____
: Week 3 _____

(Add additional weeks as needed.)

5. Although the personal satisfaction of accomplishing goals can be reinforcing, you can establish additional reinforcements (increasingly larger!) on daily and weekly levels as well as for reaching your final goal: For example, you may make a certain amount of TV watching a daily reinforcer, a movie a weekly reinforcement, and a trip to Disney World your final reinforcer (only kidding, but you get the idea!).

If you choose to use a reinforcement schedule, what is it?

daily _____
weekly _____
final _____

6. Monitor your behavior on a daily basis (number days consecutively and add additional pages as needed):

Day   Average   Comment on Progress

7. Don't be afraid to go back and adjust your initial program as needed if goals are too low or too high.

Once you complete your program, evaluate its overall effectiveness.

Reference

Merrens, M. R., & Brannigan, G. G. (1998). *Experiences in personality: Research, assessment, and change*. New York: Wiley.

Name _____

Date _____

ACTIVE LEARNING EXPERIENCE

12.2 COGNITIVE THERAPY

Cognitive therapists believe that many psychological disorders result from faulty or distorted modes of thought. If these thought patterns are modified, the disorder will be alleviated.

A cognitive therapist would help a client to identify irrational thoughts and beliefs and reinterpret the experiences upon which they are based. To give you an idea of the kinds of irrational thoughts cognitive therapists might encounter, examine and respond to the following questions (from Steven Hollon and Philip Kendall, 1980) to identify any tendencies you might have.

Automatic Thoughts Questionnaire

Instructions: Listed below are a variety of thoughts that pop into people's heads. Please read each thought and indicate how frequently, if at all, the thought occurred to you *over the last week*. Please read each item carefully and circle the answer in the following fashion (1 = "not at all," 2 = "sometimes," 3 = "moderately often," 4 = "often," and 5 = "all the time").

	Not At All	Sometimes	Moderately Often	Often	All the Time
1. I feel like I'm up against the world.	1	2	3	4	5
2. I'm no good.	1	2	3	4	5
3. Why can't I ever succeed?	1	2	3	4	5
4. No one understands me.	1	2	3	4	5
5. I've let people down.	1	2	3	4	5
6. I don't think I can go on.	1	2	3	4	5
7. I wish I were a better person.	1	2	3	4	5
8. I'm so weak.	1	2	3	4	5
9. My life's not going the way I want it to.	1	2	3	4	5
10. I'm so disappointed in myself.	1	2	3	4	5
11. Nothing feels good anymore.	1	2	3	4	5
12. I can't stand this anymore.	1	2	3	4	5
13. I can't get started.	1	2	3	4	5
14. What's wrong with me?	1	2	3	4	5

		Not At All	Sometimes	Moderately Often	Often	All the Time
15.	I wish I were somewhere else.	1	2	3	4	5
16.	I can't get things together.	1	2	3	4	5
17.	I hate myself.	1	2	3	4	5
18.	I'm worthless.	1	2	3	4	5
19.	I wish I could just disappear.	1	2	3	4	5
20.	What's the matter with me?	1	2	3	4	5
21.	I'm a loser.	1	2	3	4	5
22.	My life is a mess.	1	2	3	4	5
23.	I'm a failure.	1	2	3	4	5
24.	I'll never make it.	1	2	3	4	5
25.	I feel so helpless.	1	2	3	4	5
26.	Something has to change.	1	2	3	4	5
27.	There must be something wrong with me.	1	2	3	4	5
28.	My future is bleak.	1	2	3	4	5
29.	It's just not worth it.	1	2	3	4	5
30.	I can't finish anything.	1	2	3	4	5

If you identified some beliefs that might characterize your thinking at least sometimes, what effect do they have on your life?

Negative thoughts are self-defeating and they often make us feel powerless. According to Singer (1970), the goal of therapy is personal control, with health defined by the degree to which people experience the choices at their disposal and make choices with a sense of responsibility for them.

How can you reinterpret your thoughts and the experiences on which they are based in a more constructive way? For example, if you identified item number 1, I feel like I'm up against the world, as a thought that you have, try to identify the source of this thought. Then restructure the thought to something like, Things may not be going well at the moment, but it's not the end of the world.

References

Hollon, S. D., & Kendall, P. C. (1980). Cognitive self-statements in depression: Development of an Automatic Thoughts Questionnaire. *Cognitive Therapy and Research, 4,* 383–395. Questionnaire reprinted with permission of Plenum Publishing Corporation.

Singer, E. (1970). *Key concepts in psychotherapy.* New York: Random House.

Name _____

Date _____

ACTIVE LEARNING EXPERIENCE

12.3 EMPATHY

Humanistic psychologist Carl Rogers stressed the importance of several behaviors of effective therapists. The therapist must be genuine and honest (*congruent*), provide *unconditional positive regard*, and be able to *empathize* with clients in order to create a climate conducive to growth. To assess your capacity for empathy, complete the following subscales of Mark Davis's (1980) Empathy Questionnaire.

Empathy Questionnaire

Respond to each of the following items by circling the appropriate number.

1. When I am reading an interesting story or novel, I imagine how I would feel if the events in the story were happening to me.

    0   1   2   3   4
    does not describe me well   describes me very well

2. I really get involved with the feelings of the characters in a novel.

    0   1   2   3   4
    does not describe me well   describes me very well

3. I am usually objective when I watch a movie or play, and I don't often get completely caught up in it.

    0   1   2   3   4
    does not describe me well   describes me very well

4. After seeing a play or movie, I have felt as though I were one of the characters.

    0   1   2   3   4
    does not describe me well   describes me very well

5. I daydream and fantasize, with some regularity, about things that might happen to me.

    0   1   2   3   4
    does not describe me well   describes me very well

6. Becoming extremely involved in a good book or movie is somewhat rare for me.

    0   1   2   3   4
    does not describe me well   describes me very well

7. When I watch a good movie, I can very easily put myself in the place of a leading character.

    0   1   2   3   4
    does not describe me well   describes me very well

8. Before criticizing somebody, I try to imagine how I would feel if I were in their place.

      0   1   2   3   4

does not describe me well   describes me very well

9. If I'm sure I'm right about something, I don't waste much time listening to other people's arguments.

      0   1   2   3   4

does not describe me well   describes me very well

10. I sometimes try to understand my friends better by imagining how things look from their perspective.

      0   1   2   3   4

does not describe me well   describes me very well

11. I believe that there are two sides to every question and try to look at them both.

      0   1   2   3   4

does not describe me well   describes me very well

12. I sometimes find it difficult to see things from the "other guy's" point of view.

      0   1   2   3   4

does not describe me well   describes me very well

13. I try to look at everybody's side of a disagreement before I make a decision.

      0   1   2   3   4

does not describe me well   describes me very well

14. When I'm upset at someone, I usually try to "put myself in his[her] shoes" for a while.

      0   1   2   3   4

does not describe me well   describes me very well

15. When I see someone being taken advantage of, I feel kind of protective towards them.

      0   1   2   3   4

does not describe me well   describes me very well

16. When I see someone being treated unfairly, I sometimes don't feel very much pity for them.

      0   1   2   3   4

does not describe me well   describes me very well

17. I often have tender, concerned feelings for people less fortunate than me.

      0   1   2   3   4

does not describe me well   describes me very well

18. I would describe myself as a pretty soft-hearted person.

      0   1   2   3   4

does not describe me well   describes me very well

19. Sometimes I don't feel very sorry for other people when they are having problems.

      0   1   2   3   4

does not describe me well   describes me very well

20. Other people's misfortunes do not usually disturb me a great deal.

      0   1   2   3   4

does not describe me well   describes me very well

21. I am often quite touched by things that I see happen.

0	1	2	3	4
does not describe me well				describes me very well

Scoring: There are three subscales, each composed of seven items. On scale 1, "Fantasy," (items 1–7), questions 1, 2, 4, 5, and 7 are scored directly and questions 3 and 6 are reversed (i.e., change 0 to 5, 1 to 4, 2 to 3, 3 to 2, 4 to 1, and 5 to 0). Add the total of the seven questions.

Total "fantasy" score _____

On scale 2, "Perspective-taking" (items 8–14), questions 8, 10, 11, 13, and 14 are scored directly and questions 9 and 12 reversed. Add the total of the seven questions.

Total "perspective-taking" score _____

On scale 3, "empathic concern" (items 15–21), questions 15, 17, 18, and 21 are scored directly and questions 16, 19, and 20 are reversed. Add the total of the seven questions.

Total "empathic concern" score _____

Davis reported the following means for college undergraduates:

Scale	Men	Women
Fantasy	15.73	18.75
Perspective-taking	16.78	17.96
Empathic concern	19.04	21.67

Taken together, these three dimensions of empathy determine how deeply we can relate to others, understand their perspectives, and genuinely feel for them. How did your score compare to these means?

Do you think you would make a "good" therapist based on Rogers's views? Why or why not?

Reference

Davis, M. H. (1980). A multidimensional approach to individual differences in empathy. *Catalog of Selected Documents in Psychology, 10*, 85. Scale reprinted with permission of the author and Select Press © 1980, P.O. Box 37, Corte Madera, CA 94976.

CHAPTER 13

SOCIAL PSYCHOLOGY

Name _____

Date _____

ACTIVE LEARNING EXPERIENCE

13.1 ATTRIBUTIONS

Imagine that you have received a very low grade on an exam. Think about the possible reason why you might get this grade. What would be the *most likely* reason why you received this grade?

Now, imagine that you have received a very high grade on an exam. Think about the possible reasons why you might get this grade. What would be the *most likely* reason why you received this grade?

Answer the following three questions for *each* of the two situations separately.

1. Does the reason you cited reflect more about you (Internal) or something about other people or outside circumstances (External)?

2. Does the reason reflect something permanent (Stable) or something temporary (Unstable)?

3. Does the reason reflect something controllable or something uncontrollable?

    Situation #1
        Internal or External
        Stable or Unstable
        Controllable or Uncontrollable

    Situation #2
        Internal or External
        Stable or Unstable
        Controllable or Uncontrollable

There are eight combinations of these three dimensions.

1	Internal-Stable-Uncontrollable
2	Internal-Stable-Controllable
3	Internal-Unstable-Uncontrollable
4	Internal-Unstable-Controllable
5	External-Stable-Uncontrollable
6	External-Stable-Controllable
7	External-Unstable-Uncontrollable
8	External-Unstable-Controllable

As Bernard Weiner (1985) noted, when attributions, especially for failure, fall into a particular category, they have important implications for our psychological well-being and motivation. The *locus* of attributions (Internal or External) affects self-esteem. The *stability* of attributions is related to expectations for future performance. The *responsibility* (controllability) dimension impacts emotional reactions, such as anger or depression following failure, depending on whether they are directed outward or inward. For example, if we attribute success to high ability (Internal-Stable-Uncontrollable), it will likely lead to increased self-esteem, a sense of pride, and expectations for success in future performances. If our attribution for failure is that school is difficult (External-Stable-Uncontrollable), it may lead to an expectation for future failure, a sense of powerlessness, and anger and/or depression. Stable, uncontrollable attributions for failure may lead to the development of learned helplessness.

As you analyze your own attributions, you will get a clearer picture of how behavior influences thoughts, which further influence behavior. One reason for studying psychology is to gain this insight. A second is to realize that change is possible and that we are capable of bringing about this change ourselves.

Are these attributions typical of how you view your successes and failures? Explain.

What role do your attributions play in your life?

Are there specific areas of your life where there are clearly recognizable patterns? Explain.

How can you go about changing any attributional patterns or tendencies?

Reference

Weiner, B. (1985). An attributional theory of achievement motivation and emotion. *Psychological Review, 92,* 548–573.

Name _____

Date _____

ACTIVE LEARNING EXPERIENCE

13.2 ATTITUDES AND BEHAVIOR

David Carkenoid and Joseph Bullington (1993) devised a procedure to help understand the relationship between attitudes and behaviors. First, complete the adaptation of their "Attitude Survey" below.

Attitude Survey

Indicate the extent to which you agree or disagree with each of the four statements by using the following scale:

1 = strongly disagree
2 = disagree
3 = no opinion
4 = agree
5 = strongly agree

_____ 1.   The use of seatbelts saves lives.

_____ 2.   Our country needs to address the growing number of homeless.

_____ 3.   Exposure to the sun's ultraviolet rays can cause skin cancer.

_____ 4.   Eating a low-fat diet is beneficial to one's health.

Now complete the "Behavior Survey" below by circling the appropriate answer.

Behavior Survey

yes   no   1.   I always use a seatbelt.

yes   no   2.   I have personally done something to help the homeless (e.g., volunteered at a homeless shelter, donated money, etc.).

yes   no   3.   I use the appropriate sunscreen whenever I go outside.

yes   no   4.   I maintain a low-fat diet.

In comparing your attitudes and your behaviors, are there any discrepancies (e.g., "strongly agreeing" or "agreeing" with an attitude statement and responding "no" to the corresponding behavior? If so, how do you feel about each discrepancy?

If you had discrepancies between your attitudes and your behaviors, you are likely experiencing "cognitive dissonance"—a motivating force to "change" either our attitude or our behavior. Are you motivated to change either your attitudes or behaviors where discrepancies were noted? Why or why not?

Reference

Carkenoid, D. M., & Bullington, J. (1993). Bringing cognitive dissonance to the classroom. *Teaching of Psychology, 20,* 41–43.

Name _____

Date _____

ACTIVE LEARNING EXPERIENCE

13.3 PASSIONATE LOVE

A popular topic in social psychology is interpersonal attraction. And no discussion of interpersonal attraction would be complete without touching on the subject of love. As Hatfield and Rapson (1996) noted, "passionate love is seen as a magic elixir for finding fulfillment in life, as heady a brew as power, money, freedom" (p. 155). But what is passionate love? How can we operationalize it? Elaine Hatfield and Susan Sprecher (1986) designed the *Passionate Love Scale* to assess the intense longing for union with another. Below is a version of the scale (Hatfield and Rapson, 1993).

THE PASSIONATE LOVE SCALE

Think of the person you love most passionately *right now*. (If you are not in love right now, think of the last person you loved passionately. If you have never been in love, think of the person whom you came closest to caring for in that way.) Try to tell us how you felt at the time when your feelings were the most intense.

Possible answers range from:

1	2	3	4	5	6	7	8	9
Not at all True				Moderately True				Definitely True

1.   I would feel deep despair if _____ left me.

      1   2   3   4   5   6   7   8   9

2.   Sometimes I feel I can't control my thoughts: they are obsessively on _____.

      1   2   3   4   5   6   7   8   9

3.   I feel happy when I am doing something to make _____ happy.

      1   2   3   4   5   6   7   8   9

4.   I would rather be with _____ than anyone else.

      1   2   3   4   5   6   7   8   9

5. I'd get jealous if I thought _____ were falling in love with someone else.

    1   2   3   4   5   6   7   8   9

6. I yearn to know all about _____.

    1   2   3   4   5   6   7   8   9

7. I want _____ —physically, emotionally, mentally.

    1   2   3   4   5   6   7   8   9

8. I have an endless appetite for affection from _____.

    1   2   3   4   5   6   7   8   9

9. For me, _____ is the perfect romantic partner.

    1   2   3   4   5   6   7   8   9

10. I sense my body responding when _____ touches me.

    1   2   3   4   5   6   7   8   9

11. _____ always seems to be on my mind.

    1   2   3   4   5   6   7   8   9

12. I want _____ to know me—my thoughts, my fears, and my hopes.

    1   2   3   4   5   6   7   8   9

13. I eagerly look for signs indicating _____'s desire for me.

    1   2   3   4   5   6   7   8   9

14. I possess a powerful attraction for _____.

    1   2   3   4   5   6   7   8   9

15. I get extremely depressed when things don't go right in my relationship with _____.

    1   2   3   4   5   6   7   8   9

Scoring: Total your score for the 15 items:

Score _____

The following table will show you how your score compares to those of other college students.

Score	Percentile
129	99
122	95
118	90
113	80
110	70
107	60
102	50
98	40
85	30
74	20
68	10
65	5
51	1

The higher your score, the more intense the passion you feel in the relationship.

How does your score compare to these norms?

Passionate love has its obvious delights, and research has shown that it can even be good for your immune system! But, as Hatfield and Rapson (1996) show, it can have a dark side too. "Passionate lovers may panic when confronted with the prospect of dealing with someone they have idealized. They may suffer [feel emptiness, anxiety, or despair] when they find their love is unrequited. They may discover they are extremely jealous. They may feel mortified, miserable, stung, and bruised. They may squabble; squabbles may escalate into sharp words and even violence" (p. 166). Some of these dimensions are assessed in the questionnaire.

Hatfield (1995) also noted that we need to be vigilant. We are most vulnerable to passionate love relationships (which are most likely doomed to failure) when our self-esteem has been shaken, or when we feel dependent, insecure, anxious, fearful, or needy. Buyer beware!

How does passionate love affect various aspects of your life?

Personal:

Social:

In examining your total score as well as your responses to particular items, are there areas that you would like to change? If so, why? How can you accomplish this change?

References

Hatfield, E. (1995). Self-esteem and passionate love relationships. In G. G. Brannigan & M. R. Merrens (Eds.) *The social psychologists: Research adventures* (pp. 128-143). New York: McGraw-Hill.

Hatfield, E., & Rapson, R. L. (1993). *Love, sex, and intimacy: Their psychology, biology, and history*. New York: HarperCollins.

Hatfield, E., & Rapson, R. L. (1996). *Love & sex: Cross-cultural perspectives*. Boston: Allyn & Bacon.

Hatfield, E., & Sprecher, S. (1986). Measuring passionate love in intimate relations. *Journal of Adolescence, 9*, 383–410.

Scale from Hatfield, E., & Rapson, R. L. (1993). *Love, sex, and intimacy: Their psychology, biology, and history*. New York: HarperCollins. Reprinted with permission.

EPILOGUE

Name _____

Date _____

ACTIVE LEARNING EXPERIENCE

E.1 PERSONAL THEORY

Now that you have completed a course of study in psychology, evaluate your personal theory of human behavior. Examine the following concepts and check the three that are most important to your understanding of your "self" and your behavior.

Concepts

_____ 1. Unconscious Motives (motives that one is unaware of)

_____ 2. Finding Meaning in Life

_____ 3. Habits

_____ 4. Future Expectations

_____ 5. Autonomy (independent, self-regulating)

_____ 6. Thought Patterns (how one interprets experiences)

_____ 7. Heredity

_____ 8. Early Childhood Experiences

_____ 9. External Circumstances

_____ 10. Traits (characteristics that one displays in most situations)

_____ 11. Beliefs

_____ 12. Rewards and Punishments

_____ 13. Defense Mechanisms (strategies used to protect the self from anxiety, shame, or guilt)

_____ 14. Self-actualization (inborn drive to develop one's potential)

_____ 15. Unchangeability

Explain why you chose each concept you checked.

How do they fit together to form your personal theory of human behavior?

Does your theory fit with some theories more than others (see list in Active Learning Experience 1.1)? Explain.

Compare this list to your earlier list (Active Learning Experience 1.1). How has your course experience influenced your current view of human behavior?